# accounting

Everything you need to know to manage the success of your accounts

Martin Quinn

**Prentice Hall**
is an imprint of

Harlow, England • London • New York • Boston • San Francisco • Toronto • Sydney • Singapore • Hong Kong
Tokyo • Seoul • Taipei • New Delhi • Cape Town • Madrid • Mexico City • Amsterdam • Munich • Paris • Milan

**PEARSON EDUCATION LIMITED**

Edinburgh Gate
Harlow CM20 2JE
Tel: +44 (0)1279 623623
Fax: +44 (0)1279 431059
Website: www.pearsoned.co.uk

First published in Great Britain in 2011

ISBN: 978-0-273-73537-3

British Library Cataloguing-in-Publication Data
A catalogue record for this book is available from the British Library

Library of Congress Cataloging-in-Publication Data
Quinn, Martin, 1973–
   Brilliant accounting : everything you need to know to manage the
   success of your accounts / Martin Quinn. -- 1st ed.
      p. cm.
   Includes index.
   ISBN 978-0-273-73537-3 (pbk.)
   1. Accounting. 2. Financial statements. I. Title.
   HF5636.Q8525 2011
   657--dc22
                                                    2010041989

10 9 8 7 6 5 4 3 2 1
14 13 12 11 10

Typeset in 10/14pt Plantin Regular by 3
Printed in Great Britain by Henry Ling Limited, at the Dorset Press, Dorchester, DT1 1HD

*For Margaret and Tommy*

# Contents

# About the author

**Martin Quinn** is a lecturer in accounting at Dublin City University and a Chartered Management Accountant with many years' experience in accounting practice and industry.

For the past six years, Martin has been teaching the accountants of the future. He has a firm belief in getting the basics right first, leaving complex topics easier to appreciate. He also advises many small businesses on book-keeping and accounting issues.

Martin is author of *Brilliant Book-keeping,* and *Book-keeping and Accounts for Entrepreneurs,* both from Pearson and has contributed to a number of academic textbooks. He regularly updates his blog at http://martinjquinn. com with pieces on accounting and general business.

# Acknowledgements

Thanks as always to my wife and children.

Thanks also the team at Pearson, Sam Jackson and Rachel Hayter in particular. A special thanks to Anne and Aileen at SortMyBooks for letting me use screenshots of their software.

## Publisher's acknowledgements

*We are grateful to the following for permission to reproduce copyright material:*

**Figures**
Figure 2.12, 2.14, 2.15, 2.16, 2.17, 2.18 from SortMyBooks,
www.sortmybooks.com

# Introduction

Accounting isn't the most glamorous part of running a business. Most business owners would rather spend their time running and developing their business. But accounting is important. Without it, a business may never reach its full potential and a lack of proper accounting could even create legal or tax problems that could easily have been avoided. Not to mention that without accounting a business wouldn't be able to determine if it's making a profit or loss.

Accounting is often seen as a complex and technical subject understood only by those who have completed accounting qualifications or business degrees. But, we all do some kind of accounting in our daily lives – for example, we plan our purchases and expenses according to our budget. In business, no matter how complex accounting becomes, there are some simple principles in the background. Knowledge of these fundamental principles will not make you a fully-fledged accountant, but you will begin to understand that the subject is after all not too difficult. By applying what you learn from this book you'll be able to converse better with accountants and learn what you need to know to prepare and use accounting information to manage your business better.

The purpose of accounting is two-fold:

- First, an accounting system records the receipts and expenditures of the day-to-day activities of a business. This data is vital for the completion of things like annual tax returns. It might also be useful to lenders when you apply for a small business loan.
- Second, it provides a valuable tool for assessing and analysing the performance of your business. With just a little practice, you'll be able

to make more informed decisions about how to improve your bottom line.

In this book you'll learn the basics of accounting and book-keeping. There are four parts to the book:

- accounting fundamentals
- preparing financial statements
- using accounting information to manage a business
- interpreting financial statements.

Part 1 covers the basics of accounting. Chapter 1 introduces basic concepts underlying the accounting world, the main users of accounting information, and the formats a business can have. In Chapter 2, you'll learn how to record business transactions in what are known as the day books. Nowadays, the day books might mean accounting software rather than a 'book', but you'll see both. This chapter gives sufficient knowledge to get you going, but if you want some more detail please read *Brilliant Book-keeping*. I also introduce one of the many pieces of accounting software available, SortMyBooks (www.sortmybooks.com), and you'll see some advantages of using accounting software.

In Part 2, you'll learn how the days books are summarised in the ledgers (Chapter 3). This is the first step towards preparing several accounting reports, which are collectively known as financial statements. In Chapters 4 through to 7, you'll learn how to prepare three key financial statements – the income statement, the balance sheet and the cash flow statement. Together, these three statements provide information on how much profit (or loss) a business makes, what its assets, liabilities and capital are, and how it generates and uses cash. You'll also see how SortMyBooks can help you here too. Chapter 7 deals with the accounts of companies.

In Part 3, you'll learn some management accounting. This branch of accounting is about providing information to make decisions. You'll learn how to identify and classify the costs of a business (Chapter 8) and how to use this knowledge to plan for the future and make short-term decisions on things like sales price and volume (Chapter 9).

Finally, in Part 4, you'll learn how to analyse and use the accounts of a business in a way that outsiders like investors or auditors do. In Chapter

10, you'll learn how to spot key figures and trends by using ratio analysis techniques on business accounts. In Chapter 11, you'll learn some basic business valuation techniques which are useful when purchasing another business or selling your own. Then, Chapter 12 gives you some knowledge on how external parties like auditors and the tax authorities view and analyse your accounts.

Throughout this book, what you learn is typically referenced to a business or *for profit* organisation. But, most of what you'll learn is relevant to *not for profit* organisations such as charities or voluntary organisations. As you'll see when you read through this book, accounting information is relevant to any organisation that needs to record and report on monies coming in and going out.

**PART 1**

# The basics of accounting

# CHAPTER 1

# Some basic concepts

I n this chapter you'll learn some basic 'must know' concepts and terms
of accounting. Knowing these will help you to do your own accounts
and/or converse with your accountant in a meaningful way. What
you'll learn in this chapter will be used again and again throughout the
book, so take your time and refer back to the terms and concepts later if
you need to. Don't worry; there are no numbers to master just yet.

## The nature, purpose and role of accounting

 **brilliant** definition

Accounting refers to the recording, collating and communication of business
data, usually of a monetary nature.

This definition has three key parts. First, accounting records the transactions of a business. This means that, for example, every sale made is
recorded somewhere. Second, the data will be collated or grouped. For
example, if a business manager asked his accountant or book-keeper for
a total sales figure for a month, this would be the sum of all sales for that
particular month. Third, accounting produces information which is communicated. Accounting information is normally communicated to those
who make the decisions in a business, perhaps the owner, or to external
parties like banks. This information includes things like:

- whether the business is making a profit or loss

- what a business is worth
- how much cash is in a business
- how much a business is owed and how much it owes
- how the business is performing.

To summarise, the purpose of accounting is the provision of information to decision-makers. You'll see later in the chapter who the decision-makers are.

# Branches of accounting

Accountants have several roles in the business world. If you have used the services of an accountant you may know that accountants offer book-keeping, accounts preparation, taxation and audit services. These services belong to a branch of accounting called financial accounting.

## Financial accounting

Financial accounting deals mainly with book-keeping and accounts preparation. It is concerned primarily with the production of accounting information for people external to the business. A lot of work in financial accounting is driven by legislation like tax or company law and it is also subject to professional regulation. The information produced is highly aggregated and summarised and is normally based on historic data (e.g. total sales revenue last year). As financial accounting uses historic data, any information produced is likely to be quite accurate.

## Management accounting

Management accounting deals with the information needs within a business. In larger businesses, dedicated management accountants are employed to provide this information. Managers/business owners need information on a much more regular basis than anyone else in a business. They also need more detailed information, for example, the revenue generated by each product or customer. Decisions may also be based on information which is nothing more than a best guess or gut-feeling: for example, sales of a new product. Thus, compared to financial accounting, management accounting information tends to be unstructured, more detailed and often based on estimates. This is not to say that management accountants do not do financial accounting work – they do – but their main purpose is to provide whatever information is necessary to help make day-to-day decisions. The brilliant example below gives you an idea of the main differences between the two branches of accounting.

 **example**

Financial accountants work in a typical accounting practice. They do book-keeping for businesses on a regular basis (monthly, perhaps) and prepare accounts and tax returns at year end. Management accountants work within an organisation. They keep an eye on key figures in the business (normally producing monthly accounts) and provide *ad hoc* information as required to make decisions. They also prepare plans and budgets for the future and monitor these against actual achievements.

# Business types

The format of a business can determine the type of accounting information required. The three most common formats are a sole trader, a partnership and a limited company.

## Sole trader

A sole trader means that a business and individual look like one and same to the general public or customer, but not so in an accounting sense. If you're a self-employed person, like an electrician or plumber, then you're a sole trader. As a sole trader, all rewards of the business are reaped by you. But, on the downside, you also suffer all losses.

## Partnership

In a partnership, you're in business with one or more other person(s) and you all share the business rewards and risks. Partnerships are normally formalised by a partnership agreement which sets out what each partner does, what share of profit they are entitled to, what risks they cover, etc. Partnerships are quite common in professions like accounting, law and medicine. This is mainly because no one person will have all the skills needed to operate the business successfully.

### Limited company

Unlike the previous two formats, the word 'limited' suggests that the owners are somehow protected. The owners of a company are called shareholders (see Chapter 7 for more detail on companies). Their liability is limited to the amount unpaid on shares they agreed to buy. So, if you agreed to buy £10 of shares and only paid £6, no matter what happens to the company, your liability is £4. In a sole trader or partnership, liability could be unlimited, meaning personal assets (such as the family house) could be at risk.

## Fundamental accounting terms

Now let's look at some core accounting terms. These terms will appear again in later chapters, but do refer back here – or look at the glossary – if you can't recall their meaning.

## Assets

 **definition**

An **asset** is something that is owned or something to which rights are available, which will deliver a benefit.

Say you've just started in business as a delivery service. You may have enough money to buy a delivery van, or not. So you lease a van to make deliveries and earn some money, i.e. you receive a benefit from the use of the van. Even though your business does not have the legal ownership of the van as it's leased, it would be classified as an asset of the business. If you bought it outright for cash, it would also be an asset.

Assets are often divided into non-current assets and current assets – you'll see these terms again in later chapters. For now let's distinguish between them by looking at some examples. Non-current assets are assets which tend to be a more long-term feature of the business. Typical examples would be business premises, a delivery van or office furniture. Current assets are short-term in nature and are typically turned into cash within one year. Examples of current assets are the inventory (stocks) held in a business, money owed by customers and cash in the bank.

## Liabilities

**brilliant** definition

A **liability** is an obligation which arises from a past event.

Looking at the above definition, a liability arises from a past business transaction, for example a purchase of goods on credit. If a supplier gives you 30 days' credit, this means there is an obligation (or liability) to pay at some point after the purchase transaction occurs. You can also think of a liability as the opposite of an asset – you must give away a benefit. In simple terms, you can consider a liability as a debt you owe someone. Like assets, liabilities are classified as current and non-current. Current liabilities are normally repayable within one year, with non-current liabilities repayable after more than one year. Typical examples of current liabilities are amounts owed to suppliers, amounts owed to tax authorities and a bank overdraft. Examples of non-current liabilities would be long-term bank loans or amounts owing on a lease.

**brilliant** tip

You might find it easier to think of liabilities as claims on your business that you will have to pay at some point in the future.

## Income and expenditure

**brilliant** definition

**Income** is the gains received from the sale of products or services.
**Expenditure** is a payment or a future payment for goods or services received.

Income generally means the amounts generated by selling products or services to customers, but it might also include items like bank interest or income from investments which might be termed 'other income'. In Chapter 4, you'll learn how income is treated in the income statement. Expenditure is what you would expect it to be: expenses incurred by the business. A key is that it must be expenditure for the business, and the business alone, to be classified as expenditure in accounting. For example, the cost of a business trip to Rome is a business expense, but the cost of your spouse's shopping trip to Paris is not – even if the business paid for it. You'll see in Chapter 2 that one important expense for many businesses is called 'purchases', which refers to goods bought to resell.

## Capital

**brilliant definition**

**Capital** is the money invested in a business by its owners.

What makes up capital depends on the business format. In a sole trader or partnership, capital is the money personally invested in the business. For instance, as a sole trader you might use a redundancy payment to start a business. In a limited company, capital consists of the value of shares bought by shareholders of the company. In small family-run companies, family members are typically the main shareholders and the management team. In the case of larger companies, like Vodafone or Microsoft, shareholders may be individuals, banks or pension funds and the management team is usually completely separate from these shareholders. The capital of a business also includes profits accumulated over time (Chapters 4 and 5 will give more detail). Capital, like a liability, is a claim on the business. It is effectively money owed to the business owner(s).

## Some fundamental accounting concepts

Now that you know some basic accounting terms, let's deal with some essential concepts.

## Business entity

In accounting, regardless of business format (sole trader, partnership or company), the business is a separate entity. Let's assume you're a sole trader. Your delivery van broke down so you get a mechanic to repair it. Your lawnmower is not working well and you know the mechanic is quite handy at repairing mowers too. The mechanic repairs both your van and mower. He gives you one bill for both repairs. Is the repair of the mower a business expense? You might have guessed no and you'd be right. This is because the expense of the mower repair is not for the business entity.

Each business entity needs to have a set of accounting records. If several businesses are owned by one person, each one may be a separate entity or they may fall under a single group which produces group accounts to give a complete picture of all business activities and entities.

# Accruals concept

The accruals (or matching) concept is fundamental to the preparation of accounts. The concept simply means that income and expenditure is accounted for when a transaction occurs, not when cash is paid.

## brilliant example

A business prepares accounts to 31 December each year. A bill for electricity arrives on 5 January (after the year end) and is paid on 20 January by direct debit. The bill relates to electricity consumed in November and December. Under the accruals concept, the electricity cost would be accounted for in the accounts to 31 December. The cost relates to the period of the accounts and it does not matter when the bill is actually paid. The accounts to 31 December will show the expense and a liability for the unpaid bill.

Now let's assume you paid an insurance bill on 30 September. This bill covered the business insurance for a calendar year from that date. Should the full cost be in the accounts to 31 December? If you think no, you're right. In this example, three months (1 October–31 December) relates to the current year and nine months to the next year. Thus, three months (or 25%) of the cost would appear in the current year accounts or, in other words, the expense is reduced. The remaining (75%) is termed a prepayment and is classified as an asset. In summary, the accruals concept says that revenues should have associated costs matched against them, whether paid or not.

## Going concern concept

This concept means that accounts of an entity are prepared under the assumption that it continues to operate for the foreseeable future. If, for example, a business discontinues or is likely to, the value of some items might be affected. Customers owing money might be slower to pay, or the value of the business premises might be higher or lower than the value in the accounts.

## The accounting equation

The accounting (or balance sheet) equation is a rule which always applies in accounting. It is simply:

Assets − liabilities = capital

You know what each of the three parts of the equation represents, so here are some examples.

First, let's assume you start a business by placing £25,000 from a redundancy payment into a new business bank account. The bank account is an asset of the business and the money you invest is the capital. Figure 1.1 depicts this graphically.

Bank £25,000                    Nil                    £25,000

Figure 1.1 Accounting equation example

Both sides are equal, so the equation holds. Now, you buy some furniture and a computer for the office which costs £2,000 in total, paying by cheque from the business bank account. These are assets, and now the equation looks like Figure 1.2.

Bank £23,000                    Nil                          £25,000
Office equipment £2,000

Figure 1.2 Accounting equation example

You can see that the bank balance goes down as you wrote a cheque, but you also have new assets – your furniture and computer. Both sides are still equal. Now, let's assume you buy some goods for resale, valued at £3,000, but you get 30 days' credit. No money leaves the bank account, but you now owe a supplier £3,000 – a liability. Also, you have acquired an asset – stock – to the value of £3,000. Now the equation looks like that in Figure 1.3.

Bank £23,000          Supplier owed £3,000              £25,000
Office equipment £2,000
Stock £3,000

Figure 1.3 Accounting equation example

You can see that assets are now valued at £28,000, less liabilities of £3,000 leaving capital still at £25,000.

The accounting equation is effectively a portrayal of the balance sheet of a business, which you'll see in Chapter 5. For now, it's enough to know that this is one equation which will always apply. It can be rearranged, for example:

Assets = capital + liabilities

Sometime it's easier to remember this version and alter the wording a little to read:

$$\frac{\text{Resources of the business}}{\text{(assets)}} = \frac{\text{resources given to the business}}{\text{(capital + liabilities)}}$$

You choose which way to understand the equation and remember it best.

## Users of accounting information

Accounting information is produced with users of the information in mind. Who uses information generated by accounting and accountants? The main users are:

- You as managers/owners of a business – to, for example, evaluate the performance of a business, i.e. whether or not the business is making a profit.
- A prospective buyer/investor – any buyer or investor would want information on the assets, liabilities, profits and future plans of a business.
- Banks – if a business is to borrow money, a bank will want to see the existing liabilities and assess the ability to repay.
- Suppliers – suppliers can use accounting reports to determine whether to do business with you (e.g. grant you credit).
- Tax authorities – they need to calculate the tax on your profits.

While all the above users have different requirements, accounting information is a suitable compromise for all – it may not be perfect for everyone, but it is acceptable for most tasks. The requirements of external users, like banks, suppliers and the tax authorities are met by the financial statements, which you'll learn about in Chapters 4 to 6. While financial statements are also used by owners and managers, they also require more detailed information – management accounting information – which you'll learn about in Chapters 8 and 9.

## brilliant recap

- Accounting collates and communicates business information.

- The two main branches of accounting are financial and management accounting.

- Businesses may be sole traders, partnerships or a limited company.

- An asset is something a business owns or has a right to; a liability is a claim on a business. Capital is the money invested in a business by its owner.

- The accruals and going concern concepts are two fundamental accounting concepts.

- The accounting equation is: Assets − liabilities = capital.

**CHAPTER 2**

# Book-keeping

There are three cardinal rules – don't take somebody else's boyfriend unless you've been specifically invited to do so, don't take a drink without being asked, and keep a scrupulous accounting in financial matters.

*W.H. Auden, poet*

As the quote suggests, keeping a good record of your financial transactions is quite important. In business, keeping records of all financial transactions is *most* important. In this chapter, you'll learn the first and very important step of how to 'keep the books', or record data as business is transacted. Details of each business transaction must be captured and recorded somewhere and this information is the basis for the preparation of the financial statements of a business – we'll learn more about these in Chapters 4 to 6. In fact, recording transactions is the first step in the accounting cycle (see Figure 2.1). This chapter shows you how business transactions are recorded in a manual format first. Then, once you know how this works, you could use a software package which makes more efficient use of your time.

## The books of prime entry (day books)

The books of prime entry are the 'books' where business transactions are initially recorded from source documents like invoices and cheques. You'll also hear the term 'day books' and this is the one I like to use. They are called day books as, in a manual book-keeping system, each class of

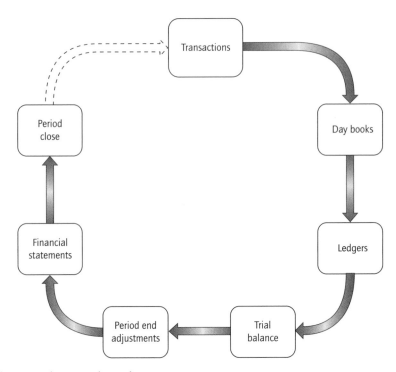

Figure 2.1 The accounting cycle

business transaction might be written in a separate hardback-type book each day. Such books are available to buy in any good office supply store and are referred to as 'analysis books'.

**brilliant** definition

The **books of prime entry** record business transactions from source documents (like invoices or cheques). They may be a 'book', or more commonly, accounting software.

This chapter is divided into the following sections:

● sales day book – this records credit sales
● purchases day book – this records credit purchases
● cash receipts book – this records cash received from customers and other sources

- cheque payments book – this records payments made by cheque/debit from the business bank account
- petty cash book – this records minor cash expenses
- general journal – this records transactions not captured in any other day book.

The data for each day book comes from various 'source documents', like sales invoices, suppliers' invoices, cheque stubs, lodgement stubs or petty cash vouchers. You'll see a sample of each day book based on a fictitious business called Highgrove Trading. The exact layout of a day book varies by business, but these examples give a good feel for what you need to know.

**brilliant tip**

Always make sure you complete or receive a source document for every business transaction. For example, always ask for a receipt or invoice for any expense and always invoice your customers straight away. It saves a lot of time later when you're trying to remember the details of the transaction.

# Value-added tax

Tax authorities like to see good records in a business, especially when it comes to value-added tax (VAT). VAT is a tax which a business collects on behalf of tax authorities. Normally, there is a turnover (sales) figure above which a business must by law register for VAT (currently £70,000 in the UK, but check http://www.hmrc.gov.uk for updates). You can of course voluntarily register your business if turnover is below this amount. Assuming turnover is above the threshold, then first you need to charge VAT on sales and record it separately in the sales day book. You also need to record the amount of VAT on any purchases expenses separately. Currently the standard rate of VAT in the UK is 20% but there is also a reduced rate of 5% and a zero rate. If you don't keep good records of VAT from day one, you might find yourself having problems very quickly. For example, a business I knew in the 1990s that did not bother to register for VAT initially ended up with a £300,000 liability within a year. The day books you'll learn about in this chapter assume a business is registered for VAT. I'll cover more on VAT later in this chapter.

 **brilliant** timesaver

As you'll see, day books consist of a series of columns into which figures are entered and totalled. Doing totals manually can be a burden, so why not use a spreadsheet. It saves quite a lot of time adding up numbers and looks neater too.

## Sales day book

In accounting the term 'sales' refers to the sale of goods or services. The term 'turnover' is also used. The sales day book records sales made on credit. The source documents for the sales day book are credit sale invoices. Most businesses make a lot of sales on credit, unless they are retail businesses. For each credit sale an invoice something like the one shown Figure 2.2 will be written up. The sample in Figure 2.2 shows a sale made by a fictitious company called Highgrove Trading to a customer called John Adams. The total amount of the sale is £600 – which is £500 + £100 VAT at 20%. (I use VAT at 20% just to keep the calculations simple.)

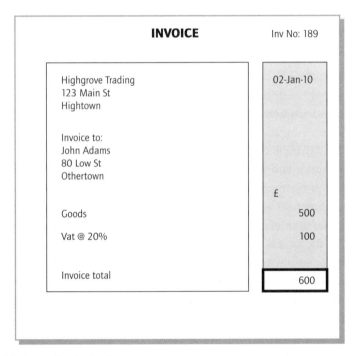

Figure 2.2 A sample sales invoice

A sales invoice can be drawn up in many ways. Some businesses often start with simple pre-printed duplicate/triplicate invoice books. You could also type invoices in Microsoft Word or Excel. Whatever your method, be sure your invoices have a sequence number and keep a copy of every invoice.

Now let's see how the invoice would be recorded in the sales day book of Highgrove Trading. We simply take the relevant information from the invoice and place it in the appropriate columns of the sales day book. Figure 2.3 shows the sales day book with the invoice to John Adams recorded.

Highgrove Trading
Sales Day Book

| Date | | Ref. | Total | Sales 20% | Sales 10% | VAT |
|------|------|------|-------|-----------|-----------|-----|
| 02/01/2010 | John Adams | 189 | 600 | 500 | | 100 |
| | | | 600 | 500 | | 100 |

Figure 2.3  A sample sales day book

This sales day book shows a number of columns. The first three reflect the date, customer and invoice number from the invoice in Figure 2.2. The total column is simply the invoice total, which includes VAT. The next two columns (Sales 20%, Sales 10%) show the net invoice amount, i.e. before VAT. In the case of the invoice to John Adams, the applicable VAT rate was 20%, so the net amount is shown in this column. The VAT amount (i.e. £100) is shown under the VAT column. You might be thinking, why separate columns for sales at each VAT rate? Well, a return of VAT must be made to the taxation authorities at regular intervals (bi-monthly or quarterly, for instance). You'll have to report sales at each VAT rate, so you need to capture this in the sales day book. Also, VAT is not relevant to the preparation of financial statements (we'll see more about these in

Chapters 4 to 6) as a business is a collector of VAT on behalf of the taxation authorities.

Of course a business will have more than one sales invoice, so I have created a few more for Highgrove Trading and recorded them in the sales day book (Figure 2.4). Notice how the net amount of each invoice is recorded under a column depending on the rate of VAT on the invoice.

Highgrove Trading
Sales Day Book

| Date | | Ref. | Total | Sales 20% | Sales 10% | VAT |
|------|------|------|-------|-----------|-----------|-----|
| 02/01/2010 | John Adams | 189 | 600 | 500 | | 100 |
| 03/01/2010 | Mark Frenley | 190 | 330 | | 300 | 30 |
| 13/01/2010 | Mary Smith | 191 | 44 | | 40 | 4 |
| 13/01/2010 | Fred Smith | 192 | 2,400 | 2,000 | | 400 |
| 23/01/2010 | Joseph Howell | 193 | 1,100 | | 1,000 | 100 |
| 24/01/2010 | Edward Jacobs | 194 | 360 | 300 | | 60 |
| 25/01/2010 | John Adams | 195 | (120) | (100) | | (20) |
| | | | 4,714 | 2,700 | 1,340 | 674 |

Figure 2.4  A sales day book for Highgrove Trading

You might have also noticed that the transaction for John Adams on 25 January in Figure 2.4 is shown as a minus figure. This means that a credit note was issued to him, perhaps for goods returned. Goods returned by customers can be entered in a separate day book called the sales returns day book, which would have a very similar layout to a sales day book. In practice, recording a return as shown in Figure 2.4 is perfectly acceptable unless you specifically want to be able to identify returns. You might want to keep track of returns if they have a high value or occur quite often. By tracking returns in detail you might be able to identify underlying problems with your product. If you're a service business, returns are irrelevant but you still might issue credit notes to customers if you over-charged a customer in error, for example.

# Purchases day book

Purchases refer to items bought for resale. Not every business will have purchases, but all have expenses. The purchases day book records goods purchased on credit. Most suppliers will provide your business with materials and/or services on credit. You might have to pay upfront for a while, but you will normally be granted credit after a few months. The source document for the purchases day books are suppliers' invoices. The layout of a purchases day book is similar to that of the sales day book and Figure 2.5 shows one that I've drawn up for Highgrove Trading.

Highgrove Trading

Purchases Day Book

| Date | | Ref. | Total | Purchases 20% | Purchases 10% | VAT |
|---|---|---|---|---|---|---|
| 15/01/2010 | Mark Henry Ltd | 300 | 600 | 500 | | 100 |
| 16/01/2010 | John's Trading | 301 | 168 | 140 | | 28 |
| 17/01/2010 | Town Suppliers | 302 | 44 | | 40 | 4 |
| 21/01/2010 | ABC Supplies Ltd | 303 | 672 | 560 | | 112 |
| 22/01/2010 | MegaSupplies | 304 | 840 | 700 | | 140 |
| 25/01/2010 | ABC Supplies Ltd | 305 | (240) | (200) | | (40) |
| 26/01/2010 | Berco Supplies Ltd | 306 | 240 | 200 | | 40 |
| | | | 2,324 | 1,900 | 40 | 384 |

Figure 2.5 A sample purchases day book

There are some differences from the sales day books. The reference column has a different number sequence. I like to keep supplier's invoices filed in a folder using a sequential number, so I label the first supplier invoice with the number 1 and go from there. Once the sequence number is recorded in the purchases day book you can then easily find it in your files. There are two columns for purchases at different VAT rates and a VAT column, as you've seen in the sales day book. I also show a credit note from a supplier (ABC Supplies Ltd) as a minus figure in the purchases day book. Again, this could be shown in a separate purchases returns day book if you wish to track returns to suppliers, for quality purposes for example.

## Cash receipts book

A cash receipts book records cash received by a business. Cash is usually lodged to a business bank account. The sources of cash for a business would typically fall in to three categories:

1 cash sales

2 cash received from credit customers

3 other cash received.

Cash sales are sales made to non-credit customers. This usually means new trade customers or the general public. For example, a building supplies shop will normally have cash sales to the public, as well as sales on credit to building contractors. Other cash received includes things like cash received from sale of an asset or interest received.

The layout of a typical cash book is shown in Figure 2.6. I've used Highgrove Trading again. The source documents for the cash book are cheques or remittance advices received from customers in the case of credit customers, or cash register rolls in the case of cash received from cash sales.

Highgrove Trading
Cash Receipts Book

| Date | | Ref. | Total | Debtors | Sales 20% | Sales 10% | Misc | VAT | Lodged |
|---|---|---|---|---|---|---|---|---|---|
| 02/01/2010 | Cash sales | | 120 | | 100 | | | 20 | |
| 07/01/2010 | John Adams | 456 | 300 | 300 | | | | | 420 |
| 10/01/2010 | Cash sales | 457 | 110 | | | 100 | | 10 | 110 |
| 13/01/2010 | Mark Frenley | 458 | 330 | 330 | | | | | 330 |
| 25/01/2010 | Mary Smith | | 44 | 44 | | | | | |
| 31/01/2010 | Refund of water charges | 459 | 10 | | | | 10 | | 54 |
| | | | 914 | 674 | 100 | 100 | 10 | 30 | 914 |

Figure 2.6 Cash receipts book of Highgrove Trading

A date, description, reference and total column is shown, as in the sales/purchases day books. After this, things are a little different. You can see columns for cash receipts from three sources: payments from customers sold to on credit, cash sales, and miscellaneous. The column labelled 'debtors' shows receipts from customers (debtors) who have been granted credit. For example, the cash received on 13 January from Mark Frenley is paying the invoice of 3 January shown in the sales day book in Figure 2.4. The next two columns show cash sales at the two VAT rates. The VAT amount associated with the cash sale is shown in the VAT column. The VAT must be recorded here as it has not been recorded previously. See, for example, the cash sale on 2 January. The 'misc' column shows cash receipts from miscellaneous sources – I've put in a refund of water charges as an example. Finally, the column labelled 'lodged' shows how much is lodged to the business bank account on a particular day. Looking at Figure 2.6, you'll see for example an amount of £420 lodged on 7 January. This amount is made up of the cash sales from 2 January of £120 and a receipt from John Adams on 7 January of £300. It's quite normal to groups several cash receipts in one lodgement. The reference number 456 in the reference column refers to a slip in a pre-printed lodgement book.

 **tip**

To help keep a record of the make-up of each lodgement, you can photocopy cheques from customers and/or keep remittance advices, staple them together and write the lodgement slip number on the front.

## Cheque payments book

A cheque payments book traditionally records payments made by cheque from a business bank account. Cheques are not the only method used to make payments from a business bank account. Direct debits, standing orders and online payments are more common nowadays, although cheques are still used. No matter, all cheques, debits, etc. can be recorded in this day book. The source of data for the cheque payments will vary depending on the type of transaction. If you use a cheque book, the stub of the cheque book will be the source – always make sure this is filled out in full. If direct debits/standing orders/online payments are used, the amount might be known in advance and can be recorded straight away; if the amount is not known in advance the transaction can be recorded as the payment is made. You could also use bank statements afterwards to find payments which have not yet been recorded in the cheque payments book. Figure 2.7 shows the cheque payments book for Highgrove Trading, with some examples filled in.

| Highgrove Trading | | | | | | | | | |
| Cheque Payments | | | | | Light & | | | | |
| Date | | Chq Ref. | Total | Creditors | Heat | Wages | Phone | VAT | Misc |
| 25/01/2010 | Mark Henry Ltd | 500789 | 600 | 600 | | | | | |
| 27/01/2010 | Electricity company | 500790 | 120 | | 120 | | | | |
| 27/01/2010 | Staff wages | 500791 | 600 | | | 600 | | | |
| 27/01/2010 | Telephone company | DD | 125 | | | | 125 | | |
| 27/01/2010 | Hill Motors-new van | DD | 5,000 | | | | | | 5,000 |
| 29/01/2010 | Taxation authorities | DD | 325 | | | | | 325 | |
| 31/01/2010 | Petty cash | 500792 | 25 | | | | | | 25 |
| | | | 6,795 | 600 | 120 | 600 | 125 | 325 | 5,025 |

Figure 2.7  Cheque payments book for Highgrove Trading

The layout of a cheque payments book varies from business to business. The example above shows the date and narrative columns as you've seen before. The reference column shows the cheque number or other reference, for instance DD for direct debit. Next is a total column followed by a number of analysis columns. The 'creditors' column shows amounts paid to suppliers from whom goods have been bought on credit. For example, the payment for £600 to Mark Henry on 25 January is paying the invoice of 15 January in the purchases day book in Figure 2.5. Other columns analyse the type of expense for each payment – for example light and heat, wages, phone and miscellaneous. The cheque for petty cash in the miscellaneous column will be explained in the next section. The VAT column in this example actually shows a payment of VAT to the taxation authorities which is a regular payment of VAT collected by the business to the authorities. I'll explain this in more detail later in the chapter. The VAT column would also record the VAT part of payments which have not been recorded elsewhere, for example one-off supplies or services not obtained on credit.

# Petty cash book

Some businesses keep a petty cash book to record minor cash expenses like tea or coffee for the office. Figure 2.8 shows an example of how a petty cash book might look for Highgrove Trading.

| Highgrove Trading | | | | | | | | | |
|---|---|---|---|---|---|---|---|---|---|
| Petty Cash Book | | | *Paid out* | | | | | | Office |
| Date | | | Date | | Vch Ref | Total | Teas | Cleaner | Supplies |
| 01/01/2010 | Balance | 100.00 | 03/01/2010 | Tea | 234 | 2.39 | 2.39 | | |
| 31/01/2010 | Cheque | 25.00 | 06/01/2010 | Window cleaner | 235 | 15.30 | | 15.30 | |
| | | | 17/01/2010 | Pens | 236 | 7.31 | | | 7.31 |
| | | | | Total spend | | 25.00 | 2.39 | 15.30 | 7.31 |
| | | | 31/01/2010 | Balance | | 100.00 | | | |
| | | 125.00 | | | | 125.00 | | | |

Figure 2.8  Petty cash book of Highgrove Trading

The example shows a somewhat different layout. There are two 'sides' to the book. A petty cash book typically uses what is called the imprest system. This means that a certain petty cash balance is maintained and topped-up at regular intervals. In Figure 2.8, the first two columns show that on 1 January, the opening balance of petty cash is £100. This is usually actual cash held in a locked cash box. The remaining columns show petty cash expenses, analysed by expense type. Each expense item is typically supported by a petty cash voucher (you can buy these at any office supplies store) and an attached receipt. The expenses are then totalled at the end of the month: £25 in the example. A cheque for this amount is cashed – look back at Figure 2.7 and you'll see one for £25. This replenishes the petty cash balance to £100.

You might be thinking this is a lot of effort for such a small amount of money and some businesses don't bother with a petty cash book. However, there may be instances where not keeping some form of petty cash system could create problems for you. Any cash payments to employees could be deemed as income and thus treated as taxable income to the employees. For example, if employees usually buy the tea and biscuits for break-time and are reimbursed this could be deemed as taxable wages unless put through something like a petty cash book. Although the amounts in a petty cash book are usually relatively small, it is often put in place as a control tool to ensure any cash is accounted for.

## The journal

This is the last of the day books. The journal (accountants may call it the general journal) records transactions not recorded in any of the other day books you've seen so far. The journal is typically used by accountants or anyone preparing financial statements (see Part 2), but it is often used to record things like corrections to errors made in other day books. Figure 2.9 shows a sample entry in the journal:

| Highgrove Trading Journal | | | |
|---|---|---|---|
| Date | Account | Debit | Credit |
| 31-Jan | Bad debts | 360 | |
| | Edward Jacobs | | 360 |
| | (Customer bankrupt) | | |

Figure 2.9 Sample journal

As you can see, the journal simply shows columns for date, narrative and debit and credit. Don't worry about the meaning of debit and credit here, I'll deal with this in Chapter 3. In Figure 2.9, I show how a bad debt (i.e. a customer debt that will not be paid) is recorded. In the example, a sales invoice to a customer called Edward Jacobs (look back to Figure 2.4) is now known to remain unpaid. A bad debt, although associated with a previous sale cannot be recorded in the sales or sales returns day books as it is not a credit sale or return. Nor is it any form of cash receipt or payment, so this only leaves the journal as the place to record the transaction. The most important thing about a journal is putting some comment about the transaction so that you (and others) can understand it in the future. In Figure 2.9, I have simply written a comment to say the customer is bankrupt.

## Dealing with payroll and VAT

Any business may have employees. If so, then additional payroll (wages) records need to be kept. I'm not going into detail here, but I do strongly recommend you use payroll software. For example, Sage and Quickbooks provide UK payroll software cheaply and by using Google I have found software called 12 Pay, which is freely available. Using payroll software will do all the complex calculating for you, which means you need only record hours worked by employees to feed into the software. I strongly recommend you use payroll software as the taxation and national insurance arrangements can be quite awkward to get to terms with in a manual system. Of course as employees are paid, the amounts paid will be entered in the cheque payments book. Also, any taxes and national insurance deducted from employees will need to be paid over to the tax authorities at some point, usually once a month or quarterly. This payment too will be recorded in the cheque payments book.

Alongside keeping records for payroll, a business also needs to keep records of VAT charged on sales and purchases. You've already seen this is in the day books. There's one further step to accounting for VAT and that is making a regular return and payment (or repayment if you're lucky), which I'll summarise now.

Let's use the sales and purchase day books earlier as an example. In Figure 2.4, the total VAT charged to customers is £674 – the total of the VAT column. In Figure 2.5, the VAT charged by suppliers is £384. This amount is deducted from what was charged to customers. The net amount, £290, is paid to the tax authorities at some future date. In the cheque payments book, the payment is £325, which we'll assume was payment of VAT from a previous month. Thus, Highgrove Trading has a liability to pay £290 to the tax authorities. It's also possible for a business to have a refund of VAT, where the total VAT amounts charged by suppliers is greater than the amount charged on sales.

That's it for the day books. Before looking at how software can help you and your business, here are some tips for keeping good day books. These also apply if you use software.

## brilliant tips

During my years as an accountant I have applied some simple tips to make book-keeping as easy as possible.

1   Invoice all goods and services sold as soon as possible. If you're busy, it's so easy to forget to invoice. By invoicing quickly you reduce the time it takes to get paid. And don't leave it too long to enter the invoices in the sales day book. If you use accounting software, you can often email invoices to customers (and post them, too!).

2   Get a receipt or invoice for all expenses and purchases. Suppliers are normally very good at providing invoices (for the opposite reason to that in tip 1). One-off purchases or smaller expenses like motor fuel are often un-receipted but try to make sure you get some receipt for every expense. In doing so, all expenses can be verified by yourself, your accountant and others (like the tax authorities) and can be easily recorded in the day books. You could try refusing to pay unless an invoice or receipt is given.

3   Do your book-keeping regularly. Otherwise you'll end up with a mountain of work to do, which in itself is always off-putting. Even if you use accounting software (see later) and don't enter transactions regularly, you're losing a major advantage which is to be able to monitor your business performance regularly. You might also not be able to keep up with deadlines for various payroll taxes or VAT returns due. I recommend you do your book-keeping at least once a week.

4   Do what is called a bank reconciliation on a regular basis – monthly is a good idea. A bank reconciliation means checking your accounting records against the bank statements of a business bank account. Doing this you will: (a) pick up any items paid in/out of the bank account automatically, such as direct debits paid out or electronic payments coming in from customers; and (b) check your day book entries (cash receipts and cheque payments books) against the bank statement and locate errors. The end result should be a matching of your records

with the bank's. It is possible that your records might not be exactly the same as the bank's records. For example, you may have written a cheque to a supplier and recorded this in your cheque payments book. The supplier has not yet lodged the cheque in their bank account, so this cheque will not show up on your bank statement as cashed. You can then 'reconcile' or explain any differences between the two sets of records.

5 Get help. If you really must concentrate on running your business and cannot devote any time to book-keeping, get some help . You might have a wife/partner, friend or family member who could help out. Alternatively, some accounting practices offer book-keeping services or there may be a book-keeping bureau in your area. Another option is to automate your book-keeping as much as possible by using accounting software.

## From the day books to the ledgers

You now know how to record business transactions in day books. So what happens next? Chapter 3 provides more details on how what is called the double entry system of accounting works. For now, it is enough to know that all transactions from the day books get to what are called 'ledger accounts'. Ledger accounts are recorded in 'ledgers'. There are three ledgers – the sales ledger, the purchases ledger and the nominal (or general) ledger. The sales and purchases ledger hold details of transactions relating to sales and purchases, grouped by customer and supplier. For example, all transactions relating to a customer are grouped – sale invoices, credit notes and cash receipts. Figure 2.10 shows how the account of John Adams would look (see Figures 2.3, 2.4 and 2.6 for the day book transactions). Don't worry about the 'two sides' for now; Chapter 3 will go into more detail.

You might find it easier to think of the account of John Adams shown in Figure 2.10 as a customer statement you would send to him to show how much he owed. Similarly too, each supplier would have an account in the purchases ledger. Again, you'll get more detail in Chapter 3.

|  | John Adams account |  |  |
|---|---|---|---|
| Sales day book | 600 | Sales day book | 120 |
|  |  | Cash reciepts | 300 |

Figure 2.10 A ledger account in the sales ledger

The nominal ledger contains 'impersonal' accounts and less detail. Only total amounts from the day books are recorded in the nominal ledger, not individual transactions. For example, Figure 2.11 depicts what is often called a 'debtors control' account. This account contains the totals of all customer transactions from the sales day book, cash receipts book and the journal from the earlier examples (see Figures 2.3, 2.6 and 2.9). Look back at the earlier examples and you will see the figures in the account are taken from the total of the sales day book, the total of the 'debtors' column in the cash receipts book and the transaction from the journal. Again, you'll see more detail on this in Chapter 3.

|  | Debtors Control account |  |  |
|---|---|---|---|
| Sales day book | 4714 | Cash receipts book | 674 |
|  |  | Journal | 360 |

Figure 2.11 A debtors control account in the general ledger

Why three ledgers you might ask? The reason dates back to when all book-keeping was manual. One person may have recorded transactions in the day books, a second person transcribed them in to the sales or purchases ledger and, finally, an accountant would take totals from the day books to the nominal ledger. This permitted a segregation of duties, which improves control. Today accounting software can do all this once the source document has been recorded in the software. Several people may still be involved, but the amount of work is a lot less and data is recorded only once.

# Daybooks in accounting software

There are many software packages available which are suitable for small and growing businesses, including Quickbooks, Sage, TAS, MYOB and many others. I use Quickbooks and a product called SortMyBooks. Both are quite simple to use and avoid too much accounting terminology or jargon. Here I use SortMyBooks to give you an idea of how accounting software can help you get to grips with book-keeping and accounting tasks.

Whatever accounting software is used, it has one clear advantage over a manual book-keeping and accounting system; you only ever need record data once. For example, if you create a sales invoice in any accounting software, the invoice goes straight to the sales day book, is posted to all relevant ledgers and will appear on the financial statements (see Chapters 4 and 5). Other advantages are the ease of reporting and time savings. In this and later chapters I show some screenshots from SortMyBooks to give you an idea of some of the benefits accounting software can easily deliver. The following sections give a brief overview of the recording of transactions in SortMyBooks (see www.sortmybooks. com).

## Recording sales and cash receipts from customers in SortMyBooks

SortMyBooks allows you to record all transactions related to customers. You can easily record sales invoices, customer payments, refunds and credit notes. This represents the sales day book and cash receipts book as shown in the manual day book examples earlier. First, let's see how a sales invoice is recorded.

Figure 2.12 shows a sales invoice I have made up for a fictitious business called Forever Flowers Ltd. To enter this, you click on an 'Invoices' icon (encircled). Clicking on the 'Invoice' icon, displays the screen as shown in Figure 2.12. The screen layout has columns which look a lot like the manual sales day book shown in Figure 2.4. There are some extra items which need to be entered, the most important one being the 'Nominal Account'. This is the account in which the sales invoice is recorded in the nominal ledger. In fact, if you try to enter this invoice without a nominal account, the software will not save the transaction – this is a fundamental

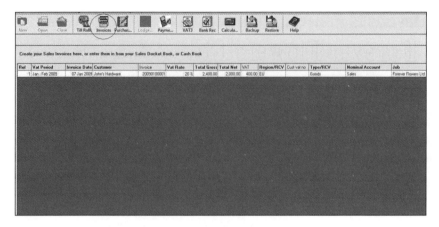

Figure 2.12  Recording a sales invoice in SortMyBooks

feature of all accounting software. When done, you can of course print out the invoice and send to your customer, as shown in Figure 2.13.

This screen looks a lot like a manual invoice and does not need a lot of explanation. You could of course add more detail to the invoice and/or customise it to include a logo and so on. There is nothing to say you must print off your invoices in any accounting software. You can still hand write them and them enter them into the software to prepare VAT returns and financial statements. But, I think you can see it's an easy task and a lot of businesses do print off or email invoices using accounting software.

Sales invoices will be paid by customers eventually, so let's see how to deal with this in SortMyBooks. Clicking a 'Lodgement' icon allows you to enter cash received from customers, and at the same time make an entry to reflect the deposit of the money in the business bank account. Figure 2.14 shows the lodgement screen.

In Figure 2.14, you can see the cash for the invoice shown in Figure 2.13 in now being received. The customer, John's Hardware, is paying the invoice in full i.e. £2,400. This cash is recorded as being a lodgement to the bank account called 'Bank Account 1'. This part of the entry is similar to the earlier examples of lodgements in the cash receipts book (Figure 2.6). There is also an added benefit here in that the personal ledger account of the customer (John's Hardware) is also updated. The next chapter will give you more detail on the ledger accounts and ledgers, but here briefly you can see that there is a tick entry beside the invoice for

# Forever Flowers Ltd

Main Street
Florville

**Vat No:** IE12345678

John's Hardware

**Invoice No:** 20090100001
**Invoice Date:** 07-January 2009

| Description | VAT Rate | VAT Amount | Net Amount |
|---|---|---|---|
| | 20% | 400.00 | 2,000.00 |

| VAT Breakdown | VAT | NET | | |
|---|---|---|---|---|
| 20% | 400.00 | 2,000.00 | SUBTOTAL | 2,000.00 |
| | | | VAT TOTAL | 400.00 |
| | | | AMOUNT DUE | 2,400.00 |

All figures shown in euros

Produced by **SortMyBooks** Bookeeping Software

Figure 2.13 A sales invoice from SortMyBooks

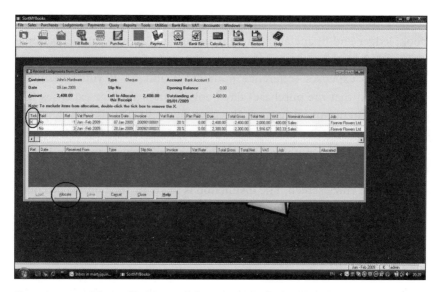

Figure 2.14  Receiving and lodging cash from a customer in SortMyBooks

£2,400, as shown. This means that this invoice is now recorded as paid in the account of John's Hardware. Clicking on the 'Allocate' button will save the lodgement, update the deposit to the bank account and show that John's Hardware now owes £2,400 less. Quite a lot in one entry, but this shows the advantages of accounting software.

## Recording purchases and payments to suppliers in SortMyBooks

Figure 2.15 shows how goods and expenses obtained on credit are handled in SortMyBooks by clicking on a 'Purchases' icon.

| Ref | Vat Period | Date | Supplier | Invoice | Vat Rate | Total Gross | Total Net | VAT | Resale | Region/RCV | EU VAT/RCV | Type | Nominal Account |
|---|---|---|---|---|---|---|---|---|---|---|---|---|---|
| 1 | Jan - Feb 2009 | 07 Jan 2009 | Janis Flowers | 12345 | Zero% | 300.00 | 300.00 | 0.00 | Resale | EU | 0.00 | Goods | Purchase for Resale |
| 2 | Jan - Feb 2009 | 07 Jan 2009 | Marys Flowers | 345R | Zero% Export | 100.00 | 100.00 | 0.00 | Resale | EU | 0.00 | Goods | Purchase for Resale |
| 3 | Jan - Feb 2009 | 13 Jan 2009 | Better Supplies | 345678 | 20 % | 240.00 | 240.00 | 0.00 | NonResale | EU | 48.00 | Goods | Other Expenses |
| 4 | Jan - Feb 2009 | 23 Jan 2009 | Viking Supplies | 123 | 20 % | 120.00 | 120.00 | 0.00 | NonResale | EU | 24.00 | Goods | Office Supplies |

Figure 2.15  Entering purchases and expenses in SortMyBooks

You can see the VAT rate and amount is shown. Look at the column at the far right. Here, as in the recording of sales, you specify the nominal account to post the transaction to. This purchase is thus posted in the day book, ledger and financial statements in one single entry. In the example in Figure 2.15, I have entered two purchases (reference numbers 1 and 2) and two expenses (reference numbers 3 and 4). If you remember, earlier I said that the purchases day book is often used for expenses (i.e. non resale) items, once they are obtained on credit. This is what happens in accounting software almost without exception. Thus, although a menu option might say something like 'enter suppliers invoice' or 'enter bill', it usually does not distinguish between goods for resale and other items in terms of the entry screen. The distinction is made by the nominal account used (e.g. purchases or office supplies). But, as you can see above, there is a column which specifies each item as 'Resale' or 'NonResale'. This is used for VAT reporting as you have to specify the type of goods bought on a VAT return.

Let's see how the above supplier's invoices would be paid. Click on the 'Payments' option in SortMyBooks and you'll see the screen as shown in Figure 2.16.

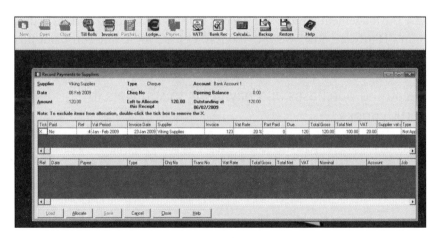

Figure 2.16  Paying a supplier in SortMyBooks

I have recorded a payment of £120 to Viking Supplies, which refers to the invoice reference 4 in Figure 2.15. This entry again covers the day book entry – a cheque in the cheque payments book – as well as updating the amount of money in the bank account in the nominal ledger and the amount the supplier is owed. In this example, I show one cheque against one invoice. In everyday business, it is more likely that one cheque will pay several suppliers' invoices.

## Recording other receipts and payments in SortMyBooks

While the vast majority of business transactions relate to customers and suppliers, there are some instances when receipts or payments don't relate to regular customers or suppliers. In addition, a business may sell for cash rather than on credit, like a retailer for example. If a business sells primarily for cash, the same procedures for recording cash received typically apply in any accounting software regardless of whether the customer is a credit or cash customer. For example, in SortMyBooks you would enter cash received from customers in the same way as shown in Figure 2.14, perhaps using a customer called 'Cash Sales'. It is also possible that a business will get one-off cash receipts. For example, in Figure 2.17 I show the receipt of £1,000 from an insurance company which is recorded in SortMyBooks using a 'All other receipts' option. You can see this is recorded to the 'miscellaneous' income account, which is like recording a receipt in the cash receipts book under a miscellaneous column. As before, the bank account will be updated with this amount and the financial statements will also show the income.

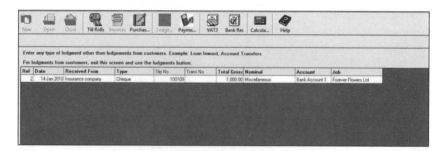

Figure 2.17 Miscellaneous cash receipts in SortMyBooks

Many payments are made by a business other than to suppliers. For example, payments might be for wages and salaries, the purchase of an asset, income taxes or rent, to name but a few. Such payments are typically entered as simple cheque payments – remember that cheques might mean direct debits or standing orders too. For example, in SortMyBooks I can use an 'All other payments' option to records payments for wages and rents as shown in Figure 2.18.

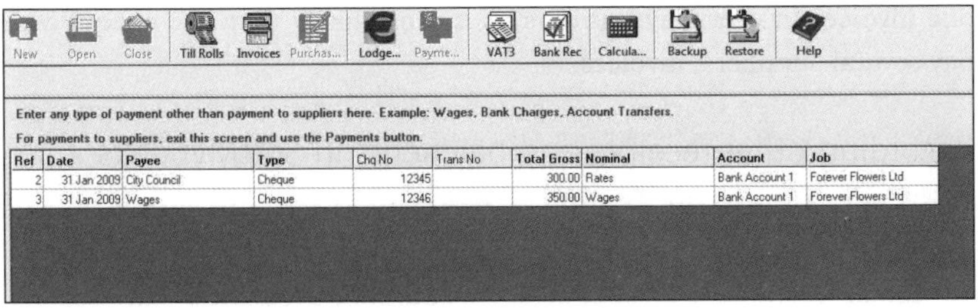

Figure 2.18  Other payments in SortMyBooks

The payments shown in Figure 2.18 equate to entering them in a cheque payments book, perhaps under a wages or rent column. As before, these payments also get posted to the bank account in the ledger and to the expense accounts, and will appear in the financial statements.

I've only briefly touched on what software like SortMyBooks can do, but I think you'll appreciate time can be saved, as once a transaction is entered it effectively goes all the way to the financial statements. Buying some accounting software is an important decision, so here's a tip.

## brilliant tip

If you decide to buy accounting software, always check the features first. There can be more than one version of software depending on the size and nature of a business, so check the feature most relevant to you. For example, will you need to trade in more than one currency? Think of the future too – how you think your business will grow, for example? Choosing the right version avoids the need to change or upgrade too soon. You should also check to ensure the software works with the operating system (Windows, Mac or Linux) your computer uses. Also check the reporting capability of the software. For example, can reports be exported to a spreadsheet for you to manipulate. If in doubt about what software features you need, ask an accountant or an existing user of the software.

## brilliant recap

- A business goes through what is called the accounting cycle, which starts with the recording of transactions and ends with the production of financial statements.

- Business transactions are recorded in books of prime entry or 'day books'. There are day books to record sales, purchases, cash received, cheques paid and petty cash. Each day book records transactions in some detail.

- A journal is a day book which records transactions which cannot be recorded in any other day book.

- Most businesses are registered for VAT and any VAT amounts must also be recorded in day books.

- The day book transactions are a data source for the ledgers and financial statements.

- Accounting software can be used in place of manual day books. Software can make your book-keeping and accounting a lot more efficient.

# PART 2

# Preparing financial statements

# CHAPTER 3

# The double entry accounting system

n Chapter 2, you've learned about the day books and I briefly mentioned that the data from the day books goes to ledger accounts. In this chapter you'll learn more about the system which underpins all accounting transactions (including the day books), the double entry system of accounting. By the end of this chapter you'll have a good understanding of the double entry system and finally understand what accountants are talking about when they mention words like 'debit' and 'credit'.

The chapter starts with a brief history of the origins of double entry accounting. You'll then learn how the system works, along with some simple rules. Throughout the chapter, I'll use examples from the day books in Chapter 2, so look back as necessary. You'll also learn how to check that the double entry system has been applied correctly using the trial balance. There are a few new terms to learn, so take your time as this is a key chapter in the book if you want to understand the nuts and bolts of accounting.

## The origins of the double entry

Written records of business transactions are some of the oldest writings that survive today, dating back to circa 3300–3200 BC. These early records were simple notations of wages paid, temple assets, and taxes and tributes to a king or Pharaoh. The first known evidence of recording business transactions dates back to circa 7500 BC when merchants in ancient Persia used clay tokens to record quantities of goods given to boatmen. The boatmen who delivered the goods downriver were perhaps not always trustworthy, so merchants placed tokens in a soft clay ball, which dried hard in the sun. The ball (or *bollae)* was handed to the boatmen. On arrival at the intended destination the boatman handed the bollae over to the buyer, who broke it open and checked if the quantity of goods matched the number of tokens. About 3500 BC, the bollae system was replaced with a system of scribing marks on a clay tablet. By about 3000 BC a full number and writing system had evolved.

What we understand today as the double entry system of accounting was first written about by an Italian monk called Luca Pacioli. In 1494 he published a book which detailed the double entry system still in use today. The next section gives the principles set out by Pacioli. Although business has become increasing complex since Pacioli's time, the system is applied in same way today.

## Principles of double entry accounting

The core premise of the double entry system is that the position and performance of a business are recorded in 'accounts'. Traditionally, accounts were written up in large books called ledgers, which gives the more commonly used name of ledger accounts. Each ledger account is a history of money values of a particular aspect of a business. For example, a sales account would record all sales-related transactions and a light and heat account would record all costs of heating and lighting a business.

The system is called the double entry system as each business transaction is recorded in at least two accounts. Before you learn how to record ledger account transactions, you need to know a little more about ledger accounts.

### Layout of a ledger account

Figure 3.1 shows the layout of a ledger account. You can think of an account as splitting a page of a book or pad into two sides.

| Account Header | |
|---|---|
| Debit side | Credit side |
| | |

Figure 3.1 Layout of a ledger account

As you can see, the left-hand side of the account is called the 'debit' side, the right-hand the 'credit' side. This is a hard and fast rule which never changes. An account also has a header, which is some name to help identify the account, e.g. sales account, purchases account, wages account. Quite often you'll see that the word 'account' in the account header is abbreviated to a/c.

Each business transaction is recorded in at least two ledger accounts and each transaction must have a debit entry and a corresponding credit entry. This means that the total money value of the debit entry for a business transaction must equal the credit entry. These two rules are crucial to the working of the double entry system. Ledger accounts are written up in a 'ledger', which traditionally was a specialised hardback book with two sides and various columns on each side. You can use sheets of A4 paper, an analysis book or a spreadsheet. The term ledger is still used to refer to where the accounts are written or stored, be that on paper in a spreadsheet, or within accounting software.

## Which side of a ledger account do I use?

In Chapter 1 you learned the key terms: assets, liabilities, capital, income and expenditure. Once you know what each business transaction entails from these five terms, you can apply the rules shown in Table 3.1.

Table 3.1 Rules for which side of a ledger account to use

| Account type | Debit | Credit |
| --- | --- | --- |
| Asset | Increase | Decrease |
| Liability | Decrease | Increase |
| Capital | Decrease | Increase |
| Revenue | Decrease | Increase |
| Expenditure | Increase | Decrease |

To help you remember these rules, I often summarise them as follows: if an asset is to be increased, you use the debit side of an account; to decrease an asset you use the credit side. The same rule applies to expenditure. Liabilities, capital and revenue are the opposite of the rule for assets.

Now let's apply these rules with some examples. Look back to Figure 2.4, where on 2 January Highgrove Trading made a sale to John Adams for £600, which was a sale of £500 plus £100 VAT. First, what types of ledger account are present in this transaction? Write down the name and type of the ledger accounts here:

_____

_____

_____

Let's see if you're right. There are three accounts: there's an account for sales, an account for John Adams and an account for VAT. Sales (referring to Table 2.1) will have a credit entry as sales increase – a new sale has been made. John Adams' account will have a debit entry as it is an asset (he owes us money) and the asset is increasing. Finally, the VAT account is a liability (it is owed to the tax authorities) and is being increased, and so will have a credit entry. Figure 3.2 shows the three ledger accounts.

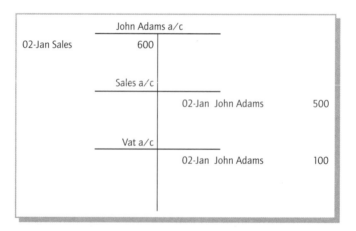

Figure 3.2 Ledger accounts for sale transaction to John Adams

Each ledger entry has the date of the transaction. You should include some narrative or reference to link the entry to the other ledger accounts. Always try to do this, as it helps anyone trying to follow the transactions in the ledger. For example, in the sales account I use the narrative 'John Adams'. The amount of each entry is also shown. In this example, the sale transaction is split up between the net and VAT amounts and the gross amount (including VAT) is shown in John Adam's account. At a quick glance you can see the sum of the debit entries equal the sum of the credit entries, i.e. £600.

Here's another example. In Figure 2.7, a direct debit payment for telephone was made on 27 January for £125. Again ask yourself what ledger accounts are involved, what type of accounts are they, and write them in below

_____

_____

This time the accounts are a telephone and bank account. Telephone is as you would guess an expense of a business, it is being increased, and is debited. Bank is an asset, is being decreased, and is credited. Figure 3.3 shows the two ledger accounts with dates, a reference and money values as before.

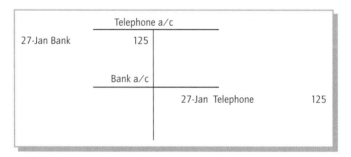

Figure 3.3  Ledger accounts recording payment for telephone services

Again you can see in Figure 3.3 that the sum of the money values on the debit side equal those on the credit side.

 **brilliant** tip

There are some phrases often used to help learn double entry rules. One example is 'debit the receiver, credit the giver'. In Figure 3.2, John Adams 'receives' goods, sales 'gives' them. In Figure 3.3, telephone 'receives', bank 'gives'. Sometimes these phrases might not work, so if in doubt, look at Table 3.1.

## Closing off a ledger account

The examples so far have used a single business transaction. Of course, multiple business transactions occur which builds up a history of the asset, expense, liability, etc. in the ledger account. At least once a year the ledger accounts must be summarised in some way to be useful in the preparation of financial statements for a business. When a summary of the ledger accounts is required, they are 'closed off'. This means that a snapshot of the money value of each ledger account is taken at a point in time. In a manual ledger system, this is usually a month-end or year-end, whereas accounting software will allow you to do it anytime. The process of closing off ledger accounts is quite simple. You need only do a little adding and subtracting, so let's see how it's done.

Take a look at Figure 3.4. This shows the ledger account of ABC Supplies Ltd. The transactions recorded are those shown earlier in the purchases day book in Figure 2.5.

| ABC Supplies a/c | | | |
|---|---|---|---|
| 25-Jan Returns | 240 | 21-Jan Puchases | 672 |
| 31-Jan Balance c/d | 432 | | |
| | 672 | | 672 |
| | | 01-Feb Balance b/d | 432 |

Figure 3.4  A closed off ledger account

On the credit side, you can see the purchase of goods for £672; the corresponding debit entry will be in the purchases account. On the debit side is a return for £240; the credit entry for this will be in the purchases account also. To close off the account, you simply follow these steps:

1 Add up the transactions on both sides of the account: in Figure 3.4 this is quite simple as there is only one entry on each side.

2 Subtract the smaller total from the larger total: in Figure 3.4 this is £672 minus £240, giving £432.

3 Enter the difference on the smaller side on the account and label it 'balance carried down', which is usually shortened to 'balance c/d'. You can see the balance carried down on the debit side of the account of ABC Supplies Ltd above. Use the date you are closing the account on as the date reference. This is usually a month- or year-end.

4 Now, both sides of the account should total to give the same amount, i.e. £672 in Figure 3.4. A line or two below where you enter the balance carried down, total both sides of the account at the same line level, as shown. It is customary to double underline the totals.

5 Finally, below the totals enter the balance carried down amount as a 'balance brought down', usually shortened to 'balance b/d'. This is keeping the 'every debit must have a credit' rule. The date for this entry is usually the first day of a month or year and is always the day following the balance carried down date.

As we'll see shortly, closing off ledger accounts is the first step in the preparation of financial statements of a business. For now, you can think of the balance on a ledger account as being a summary of all transactions compressed into a single figure. You might notice too that the side the balance brought down appears in the ledger account tends to follow the rules as given in Table 3.1 earlier. So, for example, the account of ABC Suppliers Ltd has a credit balance brought down as it is a liability – the supplier is owed money.

It is also possible to draw up ledger accounts in a three-column format. This is much easier if you use a spreadsheet to do ledger accounts and this format is often used in accounting software. Take a look at Figure 3.5. It shows the account for ABC Supplies Ltd again but in a three-column format. You can see that the balance is calculated after each entry, so a balance brought down is always available. I show a label 'Cr' to show the balance as credit, which is quite a common way to distinguish balances in these ledger accounts.

| ABC Supplies Ltd a/c | Debit | Credit | Balance | |
|---|---|---|---|---|
| 21-Jan Purchases | | 672 | 672 | Cr |
| 25-Jan Returns | 240 | | 432 | Cr |

Figure 3.5  Three column format ledger account

## Nominal and personal ledgers

I have already briefly mentioned the two different types of ledger in Chapter 2 – the nominal and personal ledger. For example, the accounts of ABC Supplies Ltd and John Adams above are personal accounts. These types of accounts for customers and suppliers are part of the personal ledgers. There are two personal ledgers; one called the accounts receivable, debtors or sales ledger for transactions relating to customers; the other called the accounts payable, creditors or purchases ledger for supplier transactions. You have learned in Chapter 2 that transactions are recorded in day books and these in turn get to the personal ledgers. All supplier and customer transactions – purchases, sales, receipts, payments and so on – are entered to a personal account from the day books. This means, for example, that each line in a sales day book or each entry in the creditors column of the cheque payments will be posted to a personal account. It is therefore possible to track how much each customer owes and, similarly, how much each supplier is owed.

The nominal (or general) ledger is used for all non-personal accounts. This ledger is more often used by accountants, while other accounting staff in a business might be responsible for the personal ledgers. Data from the day books is also recorded in the nominal ledger but not in personal accounts. Instead, totals from the day books are entered in summary type accounts called control accounts. Each personal ledger has a control account in the nominal ledger – the accounts receivable (or debtors, sales) control account and the accounts payable (or creditors, purchases) control account. You have already seen a debtors control account based on the sales day book, cash receipts book and general journal in Chapter 2 (see Figure 2.11). Figure 3.6 shows the control account again, this time properly closed off. A similar control account would be prepared for suppliers from the day books, namely the purchases day book, cheque payments book and the general journal.

| Debtors Control account | | | |
|---|---|---|---|
| Sales day book | 4,714 | Cash receipts book | 674 |
| | | Journal - bad debt | 360 |
| | | Balance c/d | 3,680 |
| | 4,714 | | 4,714 |
| Balance b/d | 3,680 | | |

Figure 3.6  A debtors control account for Highgrove Trading

The debit side amount of £4,714 is the total of the sales day book from Figure 2.4. The corresponding credit entry for this is in the sales account in the nominal ledger. Similarly, the credit side amount of £674 is the total cash received from customers in the cash receipts book (see Figure 2.6). The corresponding debit entry for this is in the bank account in the nominal ledger. Finally, the credit side amount of £360 originated in the general journal (see Figure 2.9). The corresponding debit entry for this is to a bad debts account in the nominal ledger.

So, what's the link between the nominal ledger and the personal ledger? The answer is the control account. In the example above, the customers of Highgrove Trading owe a total of £3,680. This should be the sum of the balances on all personal accounts from the debtors ledger. Figure 3.7 shows the personal accounts, so let's see. The entries in Figure 3.7 come from Figures 2.4, 2.6 and 2.9.

|  | John Adams a/c | | |
|---|---|---|---|
| 02-Jan Sales | 600 | 25-Jan Returns | 120 |
|  |  | 07-Jan Cash | 300 |
|  |  | 31-Jan Balance c/d | 180 |
|  | 600 | | 600 |
| 01-Feb Balance b/d | 180 | | |

|  | Mark Frenley a/c | | |
|---|---|---|---|
| 03-Jan Sales | 330 | 13-Jan Cash | 330 |

|  | Mary Smith a/c | | |
|---|---|---|---|
| 13-Jan Sales | 44 | 13-Feb Cash | 44 |

|  | Fred Smith a/c | | |
|---|---|---|---|
| 13-Jan Sales | 2,400 | 31-Jan Balance c/d | 2,400 |
| 01-Feb Balance c/d | 2,400 | | |

|  | Joseph Howell a/c | | |
|---|---|---|---|
| 23-Jan Sales | 1,100 | 31-Jan Balance c/d | 1,100 |
| 01-Feb Balance c/d | 1,100 | | |

|  | Edward Jacobs a/c | | |
|---|---|---|---|
| 24-Jan Sales | 360 | 31-Jan Bad debt | 360 |

Figure 3.7  Debtors ledger of Highgrove Trading

The balances brought down are as follows:

|  | £ |
|---|---|
| John Adams | 180 |
| Fred Smith | 2,400 |
| Joseph Howell | 1,100 |
| Total | 3,680 |

You can see that the sum of the balances from the personal accounts is the same as the balance on the control account in Figure 3.6. This should always be so. Sometimes differences can occur and these need to be rectified. For example, the bad debt on Edward Jacobs' account above might be known to the accountant, but he or she did not inform the person looking after the debtors ledger. This would mean the personal account of Edward Jacobs does not include the bad debt and so causes a difference. This kind of error can even occur in accounting software if not set up or programmed correctly. If it is possible to post a transaction directly to a debtors or creditors control account, then the software might not reflect this in the personal accounts. Most accounting software gets around this problem by not permitting transactions to be posted directly to any control account. Instead, all transactions must go through day books and personal accounts.

## The trial balance

You now know the basic rules of double entry accounting. If these rules are applied correctly, the total of debit entries on all ledger accounts should equal the total credit entries on all accounts. As ledger entries form the basis for financial statements, which we'll see in the next two chapters, they need to be correct. To check if you have applied the rules of double entry correctly you can prepare a trial balance.

A trial balance simply takes all account balances (i.e. the balances b/d) from the nominal ledger and lists them in two columns according to whether they are debit or credit balances. Figure 3.8 shows an example. All data in this example comes from the day books in Chapter 2, by completing the ledger accounts and calculating the balances. As an exercise, why not do this yourself to see if you get the same answer.

I have taken the balances brought down (balance b/d) from each ledger account and simply placed them in the respective column of the trial balance. For example, the debtors balance b/d is £3,680 debit, so this goes in the debit column and so on. The debit and credit totals in the trial balance are equal, proving the principles of the double entry system have been applied. When the two sides are equal, the trial balance is said to 'balance'. But, let's now ask a question. If a trial balance balances, does this mean that all figures and ledger accounts are 100% accurate? The

| Debtors control account | | | |
|---|---|---|---|
| Sales | 4,714 | Cash receipts | 674 |
| | | Journal - bad debt | 360 |
| | | Balance c/d | 3,680 |
| | 5,555 | | 5,555 |
| Balance b/d | 3,680 | | |

| Creditors control account | | | |
|---|---|---|---|
| Bank | 600 | Purchases | 2,324 |
| Balance c/d | 1,724 | | |
| | 2,324 | | 2,324 |
| | | Balance b/d | 1,724 |

| Bank account | | | |
|---|---|---|---|
| Debtors | 674 | Cheques | 6,795 |
| Utilities refund | 10 | | |
| Cash sales | 230 | | |
| Balance c/d | 5.881 | | |
| | 6,795 | | 6,795 |
| | | Balance b/d | 5,881 |

| Bad debts account | | | |
|---|---|---|---|
| Debtors | 360 | Balance c/d | 360 |
| Balance b/d | 360 | | |

| Sales account | | | |
|---|---|---|---|
| Balance c/d | 4,240 | Debtors | 4,040 |
| | | Cash sales | 200 |
| | 4,240 | | 4,240 |
| | | Balance b/d | 4,240 |

| Purchases account | | | |
|---|---|---|---|
| Creditors | 1,940 | Balance c/d | 1,940 |
| Balance b/d | 1,940 | | |

| VAT account | | | |
|---|---|---|---|
| Creditors | 384 | Debtors | 674 |
| Cash sales | 325 | Cash sales | 30 |
| | | Balance c/d | 5 |
| | 709 | | 709 |
| Balance b/d | 5 | | |

| Utilities account | | | |
|---|---|---|---|
| Bank | 120 | Cash receipts | 10 |
| | | Balance c/d | 110 |
| | 120 | | 120 |
| Balance c/d | 110 | | |

Figure 3.8  Ledger accounts and trial balance of Highgrove Trading

| Wages account | | | |
|---|---|---|---|
| Bank | 600 | Balance c/d | 600 |
| Balance c/d | 600 | | |

| Telephone account | | | |
|---|---|---|---|
| Bank | 125 | Balance c/d | 125 |
| Balance c/d | 125 | | |

| Vans account | | | |
|---|---|---|---|
| Bank | 5,000 | Balance c/d | 5,000 |
| Balance c/d | 5,000 | | |

| Petty cash account | | | |
|---|---|---|---|
| Bank | 25 | Balance c/d | 25 |
| Balance c/d | 25 | | |

Trial balance of Highgrove Trading as at 31 January

| | Debit £ | Credit £ |
|---|---|---|
| Debtors | 3,680 | |
| Creditors | | 1,724 |
| Bank | | 5,881 |
| Bad debts | 360 | |
| Sales | | 4,240 |
| Purchases | 1,940 | |
| VAT | 5 | |
| Utilities | 110 | |
| Wages | 600 | |
| Telephone | 125 | |
| Vans | 5,000 | |
| Petty Cash | 25 | |
| | 11,845 | 11,845 |

Figure 3.8 *continued*

answer is no, for a number of reasons which you need to know. Here are the most common errors which might occur but do not prevent the trial balance from balancing:

- A transaction may have been completely omitted from the day books and thus never get recorded in any ledger. For example, a supplier's invoice may have been misplaced, or a customer not invoice for goods. This type of error is referred to as an error of omission.

- A correct entry may have been made to the wrong account. For example, a sale to a customer, B Saddle, might be posted to the debit side of the personal ledger account for B Paddle. The debits and credits will be equal, but incorrect. This type of error is referred to a as an error of commission.

- An entry could be completely reversed. For example, a credit sale is posted to the debit side of the sales account and the credit side of the customers account and/or debtors control account.

- Two errors might compensate each other. For example, you may have over-added both the purchases and sales account by £500. As the purchases would normally have a debit balance, and sales a credit balance, one error cancels the other.

- An entry could have been incorrectly taken from the day books. For example, the total sales in the sales day book might read £18,000, but you misread this as £13,000 and entered it in the sales and debtors accounts as £13,000. This type of error is referred to as an error of original entry. This particular example would be found by comparing the list of balances on the debtors ledger to the debtors control account as shown earlier.

- Finally, an entry could be made to the wrong class of account. For example, the purchase of a new delivery van might be debited to a motor expenses account (expense) and not to a motor vans account (asset). This type of error is called an error of principle.

None of these errors will cause the trial balance to be out of balance, so let's see how we might locate errors in day books and ledgers.

## Locating errors

If the trial balance does not balance, a mistake has been made somewhere in the ledger entries or trial balance preparation. And, as you've just learned above, some errors occur and the trial balance is not affected. How to find errors is a bit of a problem, but there are a number of things you can do to find and prevent errors in the trial balance and your ledger accounts:

- If the trial balance does not balance, recheck the totals of each column of the trial balance to make sure your addition is correct.

- Make sure the balances from each ledger account are in the correct column of the trial balance and you have transcribed all balances correctly from the ledger accounts to the trial balance.

- If the difference on the trial balance is divisible evenly by nine, you have transposed figures somewhere. For example, you have used £910 in one place and £901 in another. This can help find differences a little quicker.

- Check that the list of balances from each personal ledger equals the balance on the respective control accounts in the nominal ledger.

- Verify your ledgers accounts with external sources where possible. This helps avoid errors of omission. For example all cash receipts and payments can be verified with bank statements; all personal accounts of suppliers can be checked against statements sent by suppliers to ensure all supplier invoices and so on have been captured.

## The trial balance and financial statements

A trial balance also has another useful purpose and that is to help in the preparation of financial statements. Take a look at the trial balance in Figure 3.8 and you'll see it is at a month-end. Although a trial balance can be prepared at any time, it is usually prepared at a month- or year-end to help prepare the financial statements. It is very useful for this purpose as it is a summary of all accounts from which we can pick (1) the income and expenses for the income statement, and (2) assets, liabilities and capital for the balance sheet. I'll explain more in the later chapters.

## Ledger accounts and the trial balance in accounting software

### Ledger accounts

In Chapter 2, you saw how accounting software like SortMyBooks can do a lot of the accounting work once a business transaction (invoice, cheque, cash receipt, etc.) is entered. Now let's see how SortMyBooks presents ledger accounts. As an example, I'll use the sale made to John's Hardware for £2,000 plus VAT shown in Figure 2.12. An extract from a report called the 'nominal activity report' is shown in Figure 3.9.

Forever Flowers Ltd

Nominal Activity Report       01/01/2009   to    31/12/2009

| Nominal | Type | Ref | | Total Gross | Total Net | Vat | Vat Rate |
|---|---|---|---|---|---|---|---|
| Creditors Viking Supplies | PAY | 1 | 06-Feb-2009 | −120.00 | −£100.00 | −£20.00 | 0.20 |
| **Creditors** | | | | **−£120.00** | **−£100.00** | **−£20.00** | |
| Debtors John's Hardware | LOD | 1 | 09-Jan-2009 | 2,400.00 | £2,000.00 | £400.00 | 0.20 |
| **Debtors** | | | | **£2,400.00** | **£2,000.00** | **£400.00** | |
| Miscellaneous Insurance Company | LOD | 2 | 14-Jan-2010 | 1,000.00 | £1,000.00 | £0.00 | 0.00 |
| **Miscellaneous** | | | | **£1,000.00** | **£1,000.00** | **£0.00** | |
| Office Supplies Viking Supplies | PUR | 4 | 23-Jan-2009 | −120.00 | −£100.00 | −£20.00 | 0.20 |
| **Office Supplies** | | | | **−£120.00** | **−£100.00** | **−£20.00** | |
| Other Expenses Better Supplies | PUR | 3 | 13-Jan-2009 | −240.00 | −£240.00 | £0.00 | 0.20 |
| **Other Expenses** | | | | **−£240.00** | **−£240.00** | **£0.00** | |
| Purchase for Resale Jans Flowers | PUR | 1 | 07-Jan-2009 | −300.00 | −£300.00 | £0.00 | 0.00 |
| Purchase for Resale Marys Flowers | PUR | 2 | 07-Jan-2009 | −100.00 | −£100.00 | £0.00 | −2.00 |
| **Purchase for Resale** | | | | **−£400.00** | **−£400.00** | **£0.00** | |
| Rates City Council | PAY | 2 | 31-Jan-2009 | −300.00 | −£300.00 | £0.00 | 0.00 |
| **Rates** | | | | **−£300.00** | **−£300.00** | **£0.00** | |
| Sales John's Hardware | INV | 1 | 07-Jan-2009 | 2,400.00 | £2,000.00 | £400.00 | 0.20 |
| Sales Corner stores | INV | 2 | 13-Jan-2009 | 1,000.00 | £833.33 | £166.67 | 0.20 |
| Sales John's Hardware | INV | 3 | 28-Jan-2009 | 2,300.00 | £1,960.67 | £383.33 | 0.20 |
| **Sales** | | | | **£5,700.00** | **£4,750.00** | **£950.00** | |
| Wages Wages | PAY | 3 | 31-Jan-2009 | −350.00 | −£350.00 | £0.00 | 0.00 |
| **Wages** | | | | **−£350.00** | **−£350.00** | **£0.00** | |
| **Grand Total:** | | | | **£7,570.00** | **£6,260.00** | **£1,310.00** | |

Figure 3.9 A sales account nominal activity report from SortMyBooks

This screenshot shows the activity on the sales account (highlighted). You can see this is not presented as a typical 'T' type ledger account you've seen so far. Most accounting software developed for businesses tend to use a simplified layout for ledger accounts. What you can see in Figure 3.9 is the total sales figure, the net sales and the VAT. You can also see the breakdown of the total figures into three separate sales invoices. Thus, in effect what you see is an extract from the sales day book and personal ledger account as well as the sales account in the nominal ledger. Quite a lot, but it is presented in a user-friendly way which makes it easier to understand for non-accountants. Now look back to Figure 3.9. You should also see a 'debtors' heading. Here you can see the money received from John's Hardware, £2,400 as shown in Figure 2.14. Again, this is shown in a simple, easy to understand format.

## Trial balance

In any accounting software, the balance on all ledgers accounts is constantly recalculated after each transaction. Closing off accounts is therefore not needed. This means you can run a trial balance at any time. Figure 3.10 shows a trial balance from SortMyBooks.

Forever Flowers Ltd

**Trial Balance, 31 December 2009**

| | Opening | Debit | Credit | Balance |
|---|---|---|---|---|
| Sales | 0.00 | 0.00 | 5,266.67 | −5,266.67 |
| Office Supplies | 0.00 | 100.00 | 0.00 | 100.00 |
| Office Expenses | 0.00 | 240.00 | 0.00 | 240.00 |
| Purchase for Resale | 0.00 | 400.00 | 0.00 | 400.00 |
| Rates | 0.00 | 300.00 | 0.00 | 300.00 |
| Wages | 0.00 | 350.00 | 0.00 | 350.00 |
| Bank Account 1 | 0.00 | 2,400.00 | 770.00 | 1,630.00 |
| Bank Account 2 | 0.00 | 0.00 | 0.00 | 0.00 |
| Cash Account | 0.00 | 0.00 | 0.00 | 0.00 |
| Credit Card | 0.00 | 0.00 | 0.00 | 0.00 |
| Creditors | 0.00 | 120.00 | 760.00 | -640.00 |
| Debtors | 0.00 | 5,700.00 | 2,400.00 | 3,300.00 |
| Owner Funds | 0.00 | 0.00 | 0.00 | 0.00 |
| Petty Cash | 0.00 | 0.00 | 0.00 | 0.00 |
| Till Account | 0.00 | 0.00 | 0.00 | 0.00 |
| Till Rolls | 0.00 | 600.00 | 0.00 | 600.00 |
| VAT | 0.00 | 20.00 | 1,033.33 | −1,013.33 |
| | 0.00 | 10,230.00 | 10,230.00 | 0.00 |

Figure 3.10 A trial balance from SortMyBooks

It looks quite like a trial balance prepared manually. You can see the list of accounts on the left, and a debit and credit column which of course total the same amount. There is also a balance column at the left and right. These represent the balance on a ledger account at the beginning and end of the period of the trial balance. The balance column totals zero, which is correct in this example as all the opening balance column is zero, i.e. zero + debits − credits will also equal zero, as debits and credits are the same amount.

Finally, I should mention that all accounting software has a saving grace in that it is impossible for the trial balance not to balance. This is because as transactions are entered, the debit and credit elements must be in balance or the software will not permit the transaction to be saved.

 **brilliant** recap

- The double entry system of accounting is used to record all business transactions.

- Transactions are recorded in ledger accounts, which have two sides called debit and credit. These accounts are written up in ledgers, which may be a book, spreadsheet or software.

- There are two ledgers, called the personal ledger and the nominal ledger.

- Each business transaction is recorded in two ledger accounts, one with a debit entry, and one with a credit entry.

- The total of all debits will equal the total of all credits. The trial balance is used to prove this.

- A trial balance is useful in the preparation of the financial statements.

# CHAPTER 4

# The income statement

If you mean to profit, learn to please.

*Winston Churchill*

In this chapter you'll learn about the income statement, which shows how much profit or loss a business makes. The income statement is also called the profit and loss account and this term is still widely used. However, in 2005 there were changes throughout the European Union which required public companies (i.e. those quoted on a stock exchange) to adopt a common set of accounting standards. While the term profit and loss account is still used, the term income statement is becoming more common, so I use it here.

You'll first learn about the income statement of a sole trader, and then about some differences if the business is a partnership or the organisation is a not-for-profit one.

## What is an income statement?

First, the quote above from Winston Churchill gives us an idea that to profit means to gain in some way. Here's what profit means in accounting:

 **definition**

**Profit** is all income less expenses of a business.

The income statement shows the profit or loss of a business for period of time; usually a month or year. It shows all income and expenses of a business or, in other words, it depicts the financial performance of a business. As a sole trader, the income statement does not have to conform to any particular layout but as you'll learn in Chapter 6, accounting standards (rules followed by accountants) and company law dictate the layout of financial statements for companies.

Let's begin with a simple example. In Chapter 3 you learned how the trial balance is a starting point for the preparation of the financial statements. The trial balance of Highgrove Trading is shown again in Figure 4.1. Let's use this to prepare an income statement. This is an easy task as all we need do is identify the income and expenses from the trial balance. I have added some notes to the right of the trial balance to show if the item is an asset, liability, income, etc. Look back to Chapter 1 if you're not sure of these definitions.

Trial balance of Highgrove Trading as at 31 January

|  | Debit £ | Credit £ |  |
|---|---|---|---|
| Debtors | 3,680 |  | Asset |
| Creditors |  | 1,724 | Liability |
| Bank |  | 5,881 | Liability |
| Bad debts | 360 |  | Expense |
| Sales |  | 4,240 | Income |
| Purchases | 1,940 |  | Expense |
| VAT | 5 |  | Asset |
| Utilities | 110 |  | Expense |
| Wage | 600 |  | Expense |
| Telephone | 125 |  | Expense |
| Vans | 5,000 |  | Asset |
| Petty cash | 25 |  | Asset |
|  | 11,845 | 11,845 |  |

Figure 4.1  Trial balance of Highgrove Trading

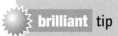 **brilliant** tip

The word 'income' typically means income from operations, i.e. income generated from what your business does. Other income, such as bank interest, is usually indentified separately in an income statement.

Looking at each item on the trial balance, the only income account is sales. The expenses are bad debts, purchases, utilities, wages and telephone. This is all you need to prepare the income statement. Before we do, here is a sample of the layout of an income statement.

**Income statement of BBB for the year ended 31/12/200X**

|  | £ | £ |
|---|---|---|
| Sales |  | 400,000 |
| Cost of sales |  | (240,000) |
| Gross profit |  | 160,000 |
| Light and heat | 1,500 |  |
| Motor expenses | 12,000 |  |
| Insurance | 3,000 |  |
| Wages | 45,000 |  |
|  |  | 61,500 |
| Operating profit |  | 98,500 |

There are a few new terms in this example, which I'll explain.

## brilliant definition

**Cost of sales** is the cost of making or buying a product for resale. For example, in a custom engineering business, costs may be accumulated for each order. More often, cost of sales is calculated only when an income statement is required. For now, think of cost of sales as the purchase price of goods you sell. Additional costs, like transport or customs duties, are also included in cost of sales.

**Gross profit** is sales less cost of sales. This is simply the profit from trading, before deducting expenses. Gross profit less expenses is the operating (net) profit.

**Operating profit** is the amount of money generated by the normal trading activities of a business. As mentioned earlier, a business may have other sources of income, such as bank interest, which could now be added to this figure.

The Highgrove Trading example does have purchases of goods, but other businesses, like a service business for example, might not have a cost of sales or gross profit at all. In fact, this portion of the income statement down to gross profit is called the trading account as it shows the profit made from trading before any expenses are deducted. Now let's take the income and expenses from the trial balance above and prepare the income statement. It would look something like that shown in Figure 4.2.

| Income Statement of Highgrove Trading for the month ended 31 January 2010 | £ | £ |
|---|---|---|
| Sales | | 4,240 |
| Cost of sales | | (1,940) |
| Gross profit | | 2,300 |
| | | |
| Bad debts | 360 | |
| Utilities | 110 | |
| Wages | 600 | |
| Telephone | 125 | |
| | | 1,195 |
| | | |
| Operating profit | | 1,105 |

Figure 4.2  Income statement of Highgrove Trading

You might notice how the income statement heading says for 'the month ended 31 January'. This makes sense, as to compare incomes and expenses over a time period means you can calculate a profit or loss for that time period. The headings of financial statements typically take the form 'who', 'what' and 'when', i.e. who is the statement for?; what financial statement is it?; and when is it for? In this example, the cost of sales figure is simply the purchases figure. However, in practice it is a little more complex than this and we'll return to the cost of sales figure shortly.

Is that it for the income statement you're thinking? Well yes in terms of the basic layout. No matter how simple or complex a business, the income statement simply lists income, expenditure and profits/losses. There are some other things you need to know, but first let's see what making a profit means for a business.

# The effect of profit on capital

Above, the income statement of Highgrove Trading showed a profit of £1,105. What does this mean for the business? It means the value of the capital of the business has increased by £1,105.

Do you recall the accounting equation from Chapter 1? It stated assets minus liabilities equals capital. In the trial balance of Highgrove Trading (Figure 4.1) there is no capital account showing, so the owner has not put in any of his or her own money. Instead there is a bank overdraft of £5,881 which is being used to finance the business. It's a bit unlikely in reality that no capital is put into the business, but let's calculate capital using the accounting equation.

| Assets | | Liabilities | |
|---|---|---|---|
| Debtors | £3,680 | Creditors | £1,724 |
| VAT | £5 | Bank | £5,881 |
| Vans | £5,000 | | |
| Petty cash | £25 | | |
| Total | £8,710 | Total | £7,605 |

Using the accounting equation, the capital of Highgrove Trading is £1,105. This is the same as the profit per the income statement in Figure 4.2 above. So, you can easily see that profits increase capital. Likewise, any losses will decrease capital. The following brilliant example provides a further illustration of the relationship between profits and capital.

---

## brilliant example

Larry's business has goods in stock which cost £30,000. He bought these goods on credit, so has a liability. Putting these figures into the accounting equation, the capital would be nil. Suppose he sells the goods for £50,000, thus making a profit of £20,000. The stock value is now nil and, assuming the monies from the sale are lodged to the bank account, the bank balance is £50,000. Putting the figures into the accounting equation we get:

▶

| Assets | Liabilities | Capital |
|---|---|---|
| Bank, £50,000 | Creditors, £30,000 | £20,000 |

You can see the capital has increased by the amount of profit made.

You might be thinking, how do the business owners obtain some of the profits from themselves? If a sole trader makes a profit, they usually withdraw some of the profits to cover personal living expenses. This is called drawings. Drawings are not the same as wages, since wages relate to employees and you can't employ yourself. Drawings are a reduction in the capital of the business and most sole traders take drawings on a regular basis. Of course, a sole trader will have to pay tax on profits and this is also a reduction in the capital of the business.

From what you have learned so far, you might have guessed by now that the profits/losses from the income statement are a link between it and the balance sheet. This is so, and we'll see the balance sheet in the next chapter. First though, you need to know a little bit more about what needs to be done to prepare an income statement. The trial balance is a useful starting point for the income statement but some further work needs to be done before we have an accurate income statement. This includes looking at accruals and prepayments, taking account of inventory on hand and calculating depreciation. We'll look at all three in turn and then revisit the income statement of Highgrove Trading.

## Accruals and prepayments

The accruals concept was introduced in Chapter 1. To refresh your memory, it means that income and expenditure is accounted for when a transaction occurs, not when paid. It is often called the 'matching' concept, too, as it means revenues and costs should be matched against each other when a transaction occurs.

In practical terms, this means that when you want to prepare an income statement, bills for expenses within the accounting period only (i.e. the period of the income statement) should be included. It is highly unlikely that all bills will have been received when the income statement is being prepared and thus need to be 'accrued' for. Also, some expenses may have been paid during an accounting period, but relate to a later period. Such 'prepayments' need to be removed. Read the following example to see if you understand the concept:

Tom's accounting year ends on 30 June. He is preparing his income statement. He discovers he has not yet received an electricity bill for June. His normal monthly bill is £800. He has also not yet received a bill for his mobile phone for the month of June, which he estimates would be £100. He rents his office for £20,000 per annum and pays this up-front on 1 January each year.

What expenses need to be accrued and what are prepaid in this example? Jot down your answer below.

The mobile phone and electricity bills need to be accrued for as they are costs within Tom's accounting year and should be matched against his income for the same period in the income statement. It does not matter if his estimates are not 100% accurate. Half of the rent (January to June) relates to Tom's income statement for this year, half to next year. Items like these are of course recorded in the day books – the general journal, in fact. Figure 4.3 shows the general journal entries in Tom's books.

You can see the telephone and light and heat accounts are being debited, or increased. This is what you would expect as the bills not yet received would increase the expense for the year. An account called 'accrued expenses' is being credited in both cases. This is a liability, or more correctly a current liability, in the balance sheet. The rent account is being credited, reducing the expense as the prepaid portion of the rent does not relate to this year. The corresponding debit is to an account called 'pre-paid expenses', which is a current asset in the balance sheet.

Tom's Business

| General journal | DR £ | CR £ |
|---|---|---|
| Telephone | 80 | |
| Accrued expenses | | 80 |
| (Telephone bill for June accrued) | | |
| | | |
| Light and heat | 50 | |
| Accrued expenses | | 50 |
| (Telephone bill for June accrued) | | |
| | | |
| Rent | | 5,000 |
| Prepaid expenses | 5,000 | |
| (Rent paid in advance on Jan 1) | | |

Figure 4.3  Recording accruals and prepayments

As shown above, accruals and prepayments affect both the income statement and balance sheet. Accruals in particular may be estimates of expenses for which bills have not yet been received. For this reason, accountants and tax inspectors keep a close eye on accruals in particular, as it is easy to 'stick in an accrual' to reduce profits. This aside, accruals and prepayments need to be addressed when preparing the income statement and balance sheet as not to do so will give an incomplete view of the true profit of a business.

## Inventory valuation

If a business buys and sells goods, it will have inventories (or stocks) at the end of an accounting year. This inventory was probably purchased on credit during the year and recorded in the purchases day book/ accounting software. What happens if inventory is still on hand at the end of a year? Will the cost carry over to next year's income statement? And, what about this year's income statement? This is another case of the accruals concept in action, as the cost of the inventory will not be expensed (or matched) against a sale until that sale occurs, and this will be in the next accounting year.

The next question then is how is inventory valued? First you need to do a count of all goods held at the end of the accounting month or year. This means physically counting all unsold goods. The effort required to do this depends on your business. Some tips on doing a good count are given in the brilliant tip below.

 **tip**

Here are some tips for counting inventory:

● Pick a time when you business is very quiet, preferably closed. This might mean some overtime for employees, but it has to be done.

● Have a sheet or printout (maybe from your accounting software) of all items you sell. This saves a lot of writing.

● Count and record all items, regardless of location, age or condition.

● Take a note of any items damaged.

● If several people are involved, create a summary of all items at the end.

● Look up the cost of all items and multiply the cost by the quantity held.

Many businesses use inventory control software, which is sometimes built into the accounting software. SortMyBooks does not have inventory software, but the basic version of Quickbooks does. If your use the stock components of accounting software, all sales and purchases of goods are recorded and you will be able to get an inventory report and use this as a basis for the count. This can save a lot of time as you need only check that what the reports says should be held in inventory is actually there.

Accounting has a rule that inventories are valued at the lower of cost or net realisable value.

 **definition**

In relation to inventory, **cost** means the amount for which the items were bought, including delivery charges, customs duties, etc. (but not VAT). **Net realisable value** means the sales value less any costs required to make the item saleable. This usually only applies to items which are damaged. For example, a furniture store might have a table that got scratched. It had cost £1,000, but can now be sold for £750. Thus, its value is £750.

Once a value has been placed on inventory, it is used to reduce the cost of sales figure in the income statement, so cost of sales in an income statement now comprises:

Opening inventory + purchases − closing inventory

The opening inventory at the beginning of the accounting period is added to the purchases figure as it is deemed a cost of the current accounting month or year. Closing inventory is deducted for the reverse reason. In both cases, the accruals concept is being applied. Inventory is also an asset; a current asset in fact. The value of inventory at the end of the accounting period is thus also entered in the balance sheet under current assets. The value of inventory would be entered in in the general journal and might look something like Figure 4.4.

| Tom's Business | | |
|---|---|---|
| General journal | DR £ | CR £ |
| Inventory − current asset | 1,500 | |
| Cost of sales | | 1,500 |
| (Year-end inventory value) | | |

Figure 4.4 A general journal entry to record inventory

The value of inventory is important since it affects gross profit. A higher closing inventory will lower the cost of sales. A lower cost of sales, in turn, means a higher gross profit. Not bad you might think, but higher profits means higher taxes. Or, if you were cynical, you might think a business could build up inventory to deliberately inflate profit or keep inventory low to reduce profits and pay less taxes.

In addition to getting an inventory value for accounting purposes, there are other reasons for performing a check on your inventories. The most obvious reason is to prevent pilferage, For example, a high-street newsagent might count some 'walkable' items daily (e.g. cigarettes, lottery tickets). Also, as inventory is an asset of a business and has a value, it should be managed as such. This means keeping inventories secure, organised, at the correct temperatures, etc., to ensure good condition is maintained at all times.

# Depreciation

Non-current (fixed) assets are used by a business to help it generate revenue and make profits. In Chapter 1, capital expenditure on assets was distinguished from normal day-to-day expenditure. Expenditure on non-current assets contributes to the revenue generated by the business, but over a period of time. A delivery truck may be good for five or more years, so how is the cost of the truck dealt with? You might guess it's reasonable to spread the cost over five years as this is how long the truck is used for. To put the cost in the year of purchase would reduce profit in an uneven way. Spreading the cost over a longer period of time seems more logical and this is exactly what happens in accounting and it is called depreciation. If you think about it, an asset gives benefits over a number of years and spreading the cost similarly is an application of the accruals concept.

 **brilliant** definition

**Depreciation** is an accounting technique used to spread the cost of non-current assets over an estimated useful life.

Depreciation apportions part of the cost of a non-current asset that has been used up in an accounting period. Or, in other words, it puts a portion of the cost of an asset to the income statement each year. It is an estimate of the cost 'consumed' over a year and is not 100% accurate. There are two common methods of estimating depreciation. These are known as the straight line method and the reducing balance method. Figure 4.5 shows how the straight line method works.

As the name suggests, the straight line method assumes an asset incurs wear and tear or loses value evenly over its life, so the cost can be spread evenly. In Figure 4.5 overleaf, the residual (scrap) value is deducted from the cost as this amount reflects what the asset might be sold for after four years and this reduces the cost. You can see that the cost of £18,000 is spread evenly over four years, so each year will see an expense of £4,500 in the income statement. Also, the charge for each year is credited to an accumulated depreciation account. This builds up each year and is shown in the balance sheet. The cost of an asset less accumulated depreciation

|                          |   | £       |
|--------------------------|---|---------|
| Cost of asset            |   | 20,000  |
| Residual value           |   | 2,000   |
|                          |   |         |
| Estimated life           |   | 4 years |
|                          |   |         |
| Depreciation per annum   |   |         |
|                          |   |         |
| Cost – residual value    | = | 18,000  |
| Useful life              |   | 4       |
|                          |   |         |
| Annual depreciation      | = | 4,500   |

Figure 4.5 Straight line depreciation method

is called net book value – which is an estimate of the current resale value of the asset.

Figure 4.6 shows an example of the reducing balance method. Using this method, the depreciation charge is based on the reduced balance (cost minus depreciation to date). This means a higher depreciation charge occurs in earlier years. For example, the depreciation is £4,000 in year one and this decreases to £3,200 in year two. Again, the relevant amount for each year will appear in the income statement as an expense and be added to the accumulated depreciation in the balance sheet.

|                                                |          £ |
|------------------------------------------------|-----------:|
| Cost of asset                                  |     20,000 |
| Depreciation to be 20%                         |            |
| of reduced balance                             |            |
|                                                |            |
| Year 1 depreciation                            |      4,000 |
| Year 1 reduced balance                         |     16,000 |
| Year 2 depreciation                            |            |
| (20% of £16,000)                               |      3,200 |
| Year 2 reduced balance                         |     12,800 |
| Year 3 depreciation                            |            |
| (20% of £12,800)                               |      2,560 |
| Year 3 reduced balance                         |     10,240 |
| (and so on...)                                 |            |

Figure 4.6 Reducing balance depreciation method

Which depreciation method should you use? The answer is to think about the type of asset. If the asset provides equal benefits, or the wear and tear is equal each year, then the straight line method might be best. For example, buildings and office furniture are often depreciated using this method. When assets become less efficient over time, the reducing balance method is often used. Motor vehicles and machinery are often depreciated using this method. You also need to think about the life of the asset, so an asset likely to last ten years with even wear and tear might be depreciated at 10% straight line. But remember, depreciation is simply an estimate and will not be completely accurate. A final point is that land is usually not depreciated – it is useful for a very long time – but buildings are, perhaps over a 50-year period.

When a business sells an asset, then the accuracy of the depreciation estimate can be seen. When an asset is sold the depreciation charge is 'corrected' and a profit or loss on the sale of the asset is calculated. Here's an example assuming that the asset in Figure 4.6 is sold at the end of year 3 for £9,500

|  | £ |
| --- | --- |
| Net book value | 10,240 |
| Cash from sale | 9,500 |
| Loss on sale | 740 |

As you can see, the asset was sold for £740 less than the net book value which means is was sold at a loss. Rather than thinking of this as a loss, you might find it easier to think of it as the depreciation estimate being out by £740. This means not enough depreciation has been charged in the accounts and this needs to be corrected by having an additional expense of £740 in the income statement. Thus, an expense for the loss on the sale of this asset will appear in the income statement. Also, when the asset is sold, the cost of the asset is taken out of the asset account as is the accumulated depreciation. This happens through a temporary ledger account called an asset disposal account. Figure 4.7 shows the ledger accounts for the sale of the asset described above – look back to Chapter 3 to remind yourself of the rules of double entry if you need to. You can see the disposal account is used to calculate the profit, which is the figure to make the account balance. You can also see how the asset and the accumulated depreciation are taken out of their respective ledger accounts to the disposal account.

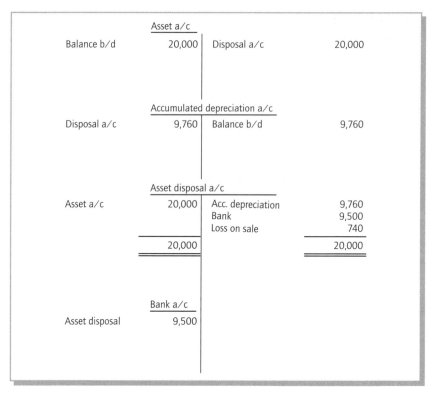

Figure 4.7 Calculating a profit or loss on sale of an asset

That's it for depreciation. The key thing is to ensure that all assets are depreciated in a consistent way each year. The depreciation expense each year will be shown in the income statement and the accumulated depreciation is in the balance sheet, which we'll see in the next chapter.

## Provision for bad debts

You already know that a bad debt is an expense incurred when a customer fails to pay a debt. However, at any point in time it is quite likely that some proportion of what customers owe will not be repaid. In this case, a provision for bad debts is created in the accounts. This provision is an estimate of the likely future bad debts. You might be thinking that if these debts are in the future why provide for them now? The answer again revolves around the accruals concept. Any bad debt, although it might not be certain until some future date, needs to be matched against income, i.e. a bad debt provision is a cost to be set against sales. Most businesses have a bad debt provision based on experience of the amount of debts which will not be paid.

 **example**

Tanya Dawson sets up a new business. She assumes that 3% of debts owed by customers will not be paid. At the end of 2009, her first year in business, she is owed £50,000 and at the end of 2010 she is owed £60,000.

At the end of 2009, a provision for bad debts of £1,500 (3% of £50,000) will be created. This amount is an expense in the income statement and is deducted from the debtors balance in the balance sheet. At the end of 2010, the provision will be £1,800 (3% of £60,000). This is an increase of £300 and this increase is an expense in the income statement for 2010. The full provision of £1,800 is shown in the balance sheet as before.

As shown in the above brilliant example, the increase in a provision for bad debts is shown as an expense in the income statement. If the provision decreased, the decrease is also shown in the income statement, usually listed with the expenses as a negative figure.

## A more complete income statement

Now let's look back to the Figures 4.1 and 4.2, the trial balance and income statement of Highgrove Trading. Having now learned some of the typical adjustments made to a trial balance, here's some more information on Highgrove Trading:

● Closing inventory has been valued at £750.

● Wages owed total £150.

● Depreciation on vans is calculated on a straight line basis over ten years.

I have included these items in a redrafted income statement shown in Figure 4.8. First, you can see that the closing inventory figure is deducted from purchases and the cost of sales figure is now lower and gross profit higher. Second, a depreciation charge of £500 is included – the van cost is £5,000 in the trial balance, which equates to £500 per year over ten years. Finally, you can see the wages figure is now £750, which is £600 from the trial balance plus £150 owed.

| Income Statement of Highgrove Trading for the month ended 31 January 2010 | £ | £ |
|---|---|---|
| Sales | | 4,240 |
| Cost of sales | | |
| Purchases | 1,940 | |
| Closing inventory | (750) | |
| | | 1,190 |
| Gross profit | | 3,050 |
| | | |
| Depreciation | 500 | |
| Bad debts | 360 | |
| Utilities | 110 | |
| Wages | 750 | |
| Telephone | 125 | |
| | | 1,845 |
| Operating profit | | 1,205 |

Figure 4.8 Revised income statement of Highgrove Trading

To summarise this chapter so far, an initial trial balance is the starting point when preparing the income statement and balance sheet. To prepare the income statement, expenses are examined to see if accruals or prepayments apply, inventory is counted and valued, and depreciation and other provisions are calculated. If you can do all this, you will have an income statement which an accountant will be quite happy with. If you can't, it does not mean that your income statement is not good enough to help make business decisions as totally accurate information is not normally required for routine business decisions.

The example income statements used so far are for sole traders. As mentioned earlier, profits made are added to the owner's capital and the owner may take some or all of the profit as drawings. You'll learn more about these movements on the capital account in the next chapter. Now let's have a brief look at the income statement of partnerships and not-for-profit organisations.

# Income statements of partnerships

The income statement of a partnership is exactly the same as that of a sole trader down to the operating profit line. After this, a statement is usually added which shows how the profit is split or appropriated among each partner. This statement is traditionally known as the profit and loss appropriation account. Also, as partners usually do not contribute equal capital and take out equal drawings, interest is often paid on capital and charged on drawings. Sometimes partners may be paid a set salary too. All the items mentioned are usually agreed in advance and written into a partnership agreement. Here's a brilliant example of a profit and loss appropriation account.

 **example**

Tom, Dick and Harry are in partnership and they have an operating profit of £130,000. They contributed capital of £100,000, £50,000 and £25,000 respectively. They receive 3% interest on this capital per annum and share profits in proportion to their capital. Drawings were £20,000, £10,000 and £20,000 respectively, and they are charged 5% interest on drawings.

Profit and loss appropriation account of Tom, Dick and Harry

|  | £ | £ |
| --- | --- | --- |
| Operating profit |  | 130,000 |
| Interest on drawings: Tom | 1,000 |  |
| Interest on drawings: Dick | 500 |  |
| Interest on drawings: Harry | 1,000 | 2,500 |
|  |  | 132,500 |
| Interest on capital: Tom | (3,000) |  |
| Interest on capital: Dick | (1,500) |  |
| Interest on capital: Harry | (750) | (5,250) |
|  |  | 127,250 |
| Share of profits: Tom (4/7) | 72,715 |  |
| Share of profits: Dick (2/7) | 36,357 |  |
| Share of profits: Harry (1/7) | 18,178 | 127,250 |

As you can see in the above example, some adjustments are made to the profit before it is divided between the three partners. Interest charged on each partner's drawings is added to the profits, while interest paid on capital is deducted. This does not mean in either case that interest is actually paid or received by a partner but rather the profits available for sharing are amended depending on the varying capital and drawings of each partner. Once these adjustments are made, the profit is then split as agreed amongst each partner and added to the capital of each partner in the balance sheet (see Chapter 5). While all this might seem a little complex, remember that the rest of the income statement for a partnership is similar to what you have already learned. More often than not, a profit and loss appropriation account will be prepared by an accountant, but you now know the basics behind it. Perhaps the most important thing to think about if you set up business in partnership with others is to ensure a partnership agreement is in place which sets out profit sharing ratios, any interest on capital or drawings, and salary entitlements. This not only helps in the preparation of the appropriation account but also avoid disagreements.

## Income statements of not-for-profit organisations

Organisations such as charities, residents associations or clubs will, like businesses, have income and expenditure. Such organisations can be classed as not-for-profit organisations as their objective is not the generation of profit. Not-for-profit organisations range in scope from a small local tennis club to a global charity like Unicef. Typically, a not-for-profit organisation will prepare an income and expenditure account which is in essence just like the income statement you've already learned. The main difference is rather than see terms like 'turnover' you are more likely to see various sources of income. Also, as profit is not the main objective, terms like 'excess income' or 'operating surplus' are more likely to be used to describe what you know from earlier as profit. Figure 4.9 shows a simple example based on a fictional cricket club.

The basic layout of the income and expenditure account shown above is similar to that of a sole trader. Income is listed first, followed by expenditure. Any surplus or deficit is added to the accumulated funds of the club, which is the equivalent of the capital account of a business.

**Aces Cricket Club**

*Income and expenditure for the year ended 30 April 2010*

| Income | £ | £ |
|---|---|---|
| Annual subscriptions | | 25,600 |
| Profit from annual dinner dance | | 1,300 |
| Grant from National Lottery | | 2,500 |
| | | 29,400 |
| *Expenditure* | | |
| Groundsman's wages | 10,000 | |
| Pavilion insurance, light and heat | 1,340 | |
| Maintainance | 285 | |
| Rent | 1,000 | |
| Accounting fees | 250 | |
| | | 12,875 |
| Surplus for year | | 16,525 |

Figure 4.9 Income and expenditure account of Aces Cricket Club

Sometimes a club or not-for-profit organisation may have some business type activity. For example, many clubs have a bar or restaurant. If this is so, then a trading account can be prepared to show the profit generated from the activity. The format of this trading account would be the same as what you've learned earlier for a sole trader. One of the advantages of preparing a trading account for a club bar or restaurant is that it acts as a control tool, where the gross profits can be monitored to ensure all sales and purchases are in order. As another example, many charities sell gifts and clothing in an effort to raise income. The income and costs of these goods might be shown in a trading account, or identified separately in the income and expenditure account. The key deciding factor on whether to show income and expenditure in a separate way (as either a trading account or listed in the income and expenditure account) is usually the volume of activity. If small, it might be grouped with other small sources of income/expenditure; if significant, it will be shown separately. For example, take a look at Unicef UK's income and expenditure accounts (http://www.unicef.org.uk/publications) and you'll see income and expenditure from card and gift sales are shown separately as the figures are approximately £2m and £1.5m respectively in 2008, which is a significant amount.

## Income statement reports in accounting software

Finally, let's look briefly at the income statement in SortMyBooks. As you might expect, an income statement report is included in all accounting software. Figure 4.10 shows an income statement (profit and loss account) of a sample company from SortMyBooks.

| Forever Flowers Ltd | | **Profit & Loss**<br>Date 31-December-2009 |
| --- | --- | --- |
| Sales | €5,266.67 | |
| Costs | | |
| Office supplies | €100.00 | |
| Other expenses | €240.00 | |
| Purchase for Resale | €400.00 | |
| Rates | €300.00 | |
| Wages | €350.00 | |
| Total costs: | €1,390.00 | |
| Net profit or loss | €3,876.67 | |

Figure 4.10  An income statement from SortMyBooks

This example simply splits the incomes statement into sales and costs. This is easy for non-accountants to understand. Have a look back to Figure 3.10, which is the trial balance of the same company. You should be able to easily see where all the items are coming from.

One of the key advantages of accounting software is how easy it is to get at the underlying information. For example, using the income statement above, within a few mouse clicks I can see the nominal ledger behind the numbers: for example, see the nominal activity report shown in Figure 3.9. This saves a huge amount of effort compared to a manual system.

On the downside, no accounting software can meet the reporting needs of all business. For example, the layout and style of the income statement shown in Figure 4.10 might not suit all. Thus, SortMyBooks and all other accounting software I know offer functionality to allow you to export reports to common office software (like Microsoft Word and Excel) to edit as you wish.

 **recap**

- The income statement shows all incomes and expenses and calculates the operating (net) and gross profits.

- The trial balance is used as a basis for the drafting of an income statement.

- The draft income statement requires adjustment for items such as the value of inventory, accruals and prepayment, depreciation and provisions for bad debts.

- The income statement of a partnership normally includes an appropriation of profits between partners.

- Not-for-profit organisations prepare income and expenditure accounts, which are quite similar to the income statements of a business.

- Accounting software provides income statement reports as standard.

# CHAPTER 5

# The balance sheet

Some day, on the corporate balance sheet, there will be an entry which reads, 'information'; for in most cases, the information is more valuable than the hardware which processes it.

*Grace Murray Hopper, Inventor of COBOL (1906–92)*

Now that you know about an income statement let's learn about a balance sheet. This, along with the income statement, are the two most common financial statements prepared from the accounting records of an organisation.

## What is a balance sheet?

A balance sheet is simply a list of the assets, liabilities and capital of a business at a point in time. This is different from the income statement; remember it covers a period of time. The balance sheet is in fact a statement of the financial position of a business, as it shows what the business has (assets), what it owes (liabilities) and how it is financed (capital). You know what assets, liabilities and capital are from Chapter 1 – look back if you can't remember – so let's see how they appear in the balance sheet.

## Contents of a balance sheet

As suggested by the name 'balance sheet', you might think something must balance. The balance sheet is actually a representation of the accounting equation presented earlier in Chapter 1, i.e. assets less liabilities equals capital. Therefore by definition the balance sheet will balance if it is a listing of these items. Or, think about what you already know about the trial balance and how it is used to prepare financial statements:

1  You begin with a trial balance that balances.

2  All income and expenses in the trial balance are presented on the income statement and a profit or loss is calculated.

3  This profit is taken to the balance sheet – added to capital, you know from Chapter 4 – with all remaining items from the trial balance.

4  Thus, the balance sheet would have to balance as the profit figure is simply the sum of income less expenses from the trial balance.

Of course as you know, there are adjustments made to the trial balance such as those mentioned in Chapter 4 – inventory, accruals, depreciation, etc. These too though are effectively double entries in the ledgers and keep the trial balance in balance: remember, for example, that an accrual increase an expense (debit) and creates a liability (credit).

Before you learn the layout of a balance sheet, you first need to know how assets and liabilities are grouped for the purposes of the balance sheet. Again, refer back to Chapter 1 if you're unsure of the basic definition of assets and liabilities, as you'll learn a little more here.

## Current assets

### brilliant definition

A **current asset** is one which is readily convertible into cash.

Current assets are more short-term in nature. They normally have some of the following characteristics:

● They are held for use or resale by the business as part of normal day-to-day operations.

● They are normally sold within one year.

● They are equivalent to cash (i.e. can be sold for cash quickly).

The most common current assets are inventories (stocks), amounts owed by customers (trade receivables/debtors), cash in hand or cash in a bank account. The level of each held depends on the nature of the business. For example, a service business is unlikely to have any inventories and a corner store is likely to have little or nothing owed by customers.

## Non-current assets

 **brilliant** definition

A **non-current asset** is one which is not readily convertible into cash or not expected to be converted to cash in the short term, i.e. within one year.

Non-current (or fixed) assets are held by a business for the longer term and usually have a productive use. Examples would be premises, vans and office furniture. What is classified as a non-current asset depends too on the nature of the business. For example, a car may be a non-current asset of your business, but would be a current asset (i.e. inventory) of a car manufacturer.

Another important point on non-current assets is that it must be possible to readily identify their cost. Look back at the quote at the start of this chapter. I'm sure you'll agree that things like information and people are of long-term benefit to a business. For example, over time the staff of any business build up what is commonly described as 'know-how' which makes them better at doing particular things than other businesses. While very important and no doubt contributing to the profitability of the business, in accounting it is not possible to put a reliable and verifiable value on such 'assets'. So, unless a non-current asset can have a reliable cost determined it is not an asset which will appear on a balance sheet. Over the years this has caused many debates in the business world, particularly in relation to brands we all know like Coca-Cola, Nike, etc. But, as brands do not have an easily identifiable cost, they are not assets. Why the fuss you might ask? Well, according to *USA Today* on 18 September 2009, the Coca-Cola brand was valued at $68bn. Just think about how good that would make a balance sheet look. Remember the accounting equation; if assets increase by $68bn so does capital.

## Current liabilities

**brilliant** definition

A **current liability** is one which will be settled in the short term, typically within one year.

As in the definition above, current liabilities are amounts owed which are due to be paid within one year. To be more precise, they normally meet one of the following criteria:

- They are paid within the normal course of business.
- They are paid within one year of the balance sheet date.
- There is no right to extend the settlement period beyond one year.

Examples of current liabilities are amounts owing to suppliers (trade payables/creditors), amounts owing to tax authorities, a bank overdraft and accrued expenses.

## Non-current liabilities

**brilliant** definition

A **non-current liability** is one which will not be settled within one year.

Non-current liabilities are liabilities other than current liabilities. Typical examples are long-term bank loans. Quite often, a balance sheet will show bank loans split into the portion due within one year, which is shown as a current liability, and the portion due after one year, shown as a non-current liability.

Now that you know a little more about the main elements of a balance sheet, let's see an example.

# Layout of a sole trader's balance sheet

A balance sheet is normally presented in a vertical layout, as shown in Figure 5.1. This layout shows assets grouped on the top portion of the balance sheet, and capital and liabilities on the bottom portion. The term 'financed by' is normally used to describe the capital section in a sole trader's balance sheet.

| Balance Sheet of J Sample as at 31/12/2010 | | |
|---|---|---|
| **Non-current assets** | £000 | £000 |
| Property | | 155 |
| Plant & equipment | | 56 |
| Motor van | | 34 |
| | | 245 |
| **Current assets** | | |
| Inventories | 145 | |
| Trade receivables | 15 | |
| Cash at bank | 46 | |
| | | 206 |
| | | 451 |
| **Financed by:** | | |
| Owner's capital | 250 | |
| Drawings | (50) | 200 |
| **Non-current liabilities** | | |
| Long-term bank loan | | 35 |
| **Current liabilities** | | |
| Trade payables | 166 | |
| Taxation owing | 50 | 216 |
| | | 451 |

Figure 5.1  A sample balance sheet

As you can see, the total of the assets is equal to the total of liabilities plus capital, so the balance sheet balances. Figure 5.2 shows an alternative way to present the balance sheet which is still commonly used.

In Figure 5.2, you can see that assets less liabilities give one balance sheet total, capital the other. Regardless of layout, both are representations of the accounting equation. You might have noticed the term 'working capital' in Figure 5.2. Working capital refers to current assets less current liabilities. You'll learn more about working capital in Chapter 10.

Balance Sheet of J Sample as at 31/12/2010

| Non-current assets | £000 | £000 | £000 |
|---|---|---|---|
| Property | | | 155 |
| Plant & equipment | | | 56 |
| Motor van | | | 34 |
| | | | 245 |
| **Current assets** | | | |
| Inventories | 145 | | |
| Trade receivables | 15 | | |
| Cash at bank | 46 | | |
| | | 206 | |
| **Current liabilities** | | | |
| Trade payables | 166 | | |
| Taxation owing | 50 | 216 | |
| Working capital | | | (10) |
| **Non-current liabilities** | | | |
| Long-term bank loan | | | (35) |
| | | | 200 |
| **Financed by:** | | | 250 |
| Owner's capital | | | (50) |
| Drawings | | | 200 |

Figure 5.2 An alternative balance sheet layout

Let's return to the Highgrove Trading example used in earlier chapters. The trial balance given in Figure 4.1 is reproduced in Figure 5.3.

Remember too we also had the following adjustments to the trial balance in Chapter 4:

- closing stock (inventory) has been valued at £750
- wages owed total £150
- depreciation on vans is calculated on a straight line basis over ten years.

From the trial balance and these adjustments, the balance sheet of Highgrove Trading is shown in Figure 5.4.

I've presented this balance sheet with assets on the upper portion and liabilities on the lower. The assets and liabilities have been taken from the trial balance and the given adjustments, i.e. depreciation, closing stocks

Trial Balance of Highgrove Trading as at 31 January

| | Debit £ | Credit £ | |
|---|---|---|---|
| Debtors | 3,680 | | Asset |
| Creditors | | 1,724 | Liability |
| Bank | | 5,881 | Liability |
| Bad debts | 360 | | Expense |
| Sales | | 4,240 | Income |
| Purchases | 1,940 | | Expense |
| VAT | 5 | | Asset |
| Utilities | 110 | | Expense |
| Wages | 600 | | Expense |
| Telephone | 125 | | Expense |
| Vans | 5,000 | | Asset |
| Petty cash | 25 | | Asset |
| | 11,845 | 11,845 | |

Figure 5.3  Trial balance of Highgrove Trading

Balance Sheet of Highgrove Trading as at 31 January

| | £000 | £000 |
|---|---|---|
| **Non-current assets** | | |
| Motor van at cost | | 5,000 |
| Accumulated depreciation | | (500) |
| Net book value | | 4,500 |
| | | |
| **Current assets** | | |
| Stocks | 750 | |
| Debtors | 3,680 | |
| Petty cash | 25 | |
| VAT | 5 | |
| | | 4,460 |
| | | 8,960 |
| | | |
| **Financed by:** | | |
| Owner's capital at start of year | | – |
| Profit for year | | 1,205  (See Figure 4.8) |
| | | 1,205 |
| **Current liabilities** | | |
| Creditors | 1,724 | |
| Bank overdraft | 5,881 | |
| Wages accrual | 150 | 7,755 |
| | | 8,960 |

Figure 5.4  Balance sheet of Highgrove Trading

and the accrual for wages. The profit from the earlier income statement
(Figure 4.8) is shown under the capital heading. As there was no capital
invested directly by the owners in the example, the profit is the only item

shown under this heading. The total capital as per this balance sheet (i.e. £1,205) will be the capital figure in the balance sheet of the next period and future profits are added to it. The capital section of any balance sheet is quite important so the next section provides some more detail.

## The capital account

In the example of Highgrove Trading (see Figure 5.4), the owners did not contribute any capital to start the business. This is not likely in reality, as most business owners will be required to contribute some personal funds to start the business – even if bank finance is available. If your business operates as a sole trader or partnership, you'll have contributed funds to get the business off the ground, or added more capital later. Normally, as a business make profits the owners take some money for themselves and this is called drawings. Also, tax needs to be paid on profits. All these are movements on the capital account of a sole trader or partnership. (I'll mention more on partnerships in the next section.)

Here's an example of the typical movements on a capital account.

 **example**

Regina sets up in business by lodging £20,000 from a redundancy claim in a business bank account on 1 January 2009. Her profits for 2009 (her first year) are £23,000, from which she pays £3,000 in tax and takes £15,000 for her own personal use. In 2010, her profits are £35,000, tax £6,000 and she takes £20,000 for her own use.

In the ledger accounts of Regina's business, this would be shown as in Figure 5.5 (for convenience I am using the end of year as the date of all transactions).

In Figure 5.5 you can see that the income tax and drawings are reflected in the capital account each year, reducing the amount of capital in the business. The capital introduced and profits made each year are added to capital.

You don't see capital accounts presented like the brilliant example above in the balance sheet of a sole trader. Normally, just the balance on the capital account is shown with the details given in a note to the accounts.

Capital a/c

| | | | |
|---|---|---|---|
| 31/12/2009 Drawings | 15,000 | 01/01/2009 Bank | 20,000 |
| 31/12/2009 Income tax | 3,000 | 31/12/2009 Profit for year | 23,000 |
| 31/12/2009 Balance c/d | 25,000 | | |
| | 43,000 | | 43,000 |
| 31/12/2010 Drawings | 15,000 | 01/01/2010 Balance b/d | 25,000 |
| 31/12/2010 Income tax | 6,000 | 31/12/2010 Profit for year | 35,000 |
| 31/12/2010 Balance c/d | 39,000 | | |
| | 60,000 | | 60,000 |

Income tax a/c

| | | | |
|---|---|---|---|
| 31/12/2009 Bank | 3,000 | 31/12/2009 Capital | 3,000 |
| 31/12/2010 Bank | 6,000 | 31/12/2010 Capital | 6,000 |

Drawings a/c

| | | | |
|---|---|---|---|
| 31/12/2009 Bank | 15,000 | 31/12/2009 Capital | 15,000 |
| 31/12/2010 Bank | 20,000 | 31/12/2010 Capital | 20,000 |

**Figure 5.5 Extract from Regina's ledger**

Figure 5.6 shows an example of a note showing the movements of the capital of Regina's business for 2010.

*Notes to the accounts of Regina*

| **Movements on capital** | £ |
|---|---|
| Capital as of 1/1/2010 | 25,000 |
| Add: Profit for year | 35,000 |
| Less: Drawings | (15,000) |
| Income tax | (6,000) |
| Capital as of 31/12/2010 | 39,000 |

**Figure 5.6 Movements on capital account note to accounts**

This note (Figure 5.6) shows exactly the same information as the ledger account above in Figure 5.5, but in a more presentable way. Typically, such a note will accompany the income statement and balance sheet of a sole trader. This note gives useful additional information on how the capital of a company is being utilised. For example, banks or the tax authorities might be interested in the level of drawings – the former to assess monies available to repay loans, the latter to assess the level of income.

# Balance sheets of other entities

## Balance sheet of partnerships

The balance sheet of a partnership is very similar to that of a sole trader. The main difference is in that each partner has a capital account and these are usually shown separately. Figure 5.7 shows an extract from a partnership balance sheet.

| Financed by: | £ |
|---|---|
| Partners' capital | |
| | |
| Partner A | 40,000 |
| Partner B | 45,000 |
| | 85,000 |

Figure 5.7  Extract from a partnership balance sheet

Partnerships often use the capital accounts to record only capital paid in or out of the partnership, e.g. on a partner joining or retiring. All other items such as drawings, interest on capital and drawings, share of profits and partners' salaries (see Chapter 4 also) are recorded in a 'current' account for each partner. If this is so, you might see both capital and current accounts in the balance sheet.

Sometimes, partners may loan money to the partnership too. If this happens, you might see a loan under the current liabilities heading in the partnership balance sheet. Other than this, and the split of partners' capital into separate capital accounts, the balance sheet is pretty much as you have learned so far in this chapter.

## Balance sheet of not-for-profit organisations

You already know from Chapter 4 that not-for-profit organisations use income and expenditure accounts and may have a surplus or deficit each year. As you might guess, such organisations don't have capital in the same sense as sole traders or partnerships. Instead, the term used is accumulated fund.

**brilliant** definition

Accumulated fund refers to the surplus of income accumulated by a not-for-profit organisation over time.

Not-for-profit organisations don't have drawings and are usually not subject to taxation. Therefore, the accumulated fund is the sum of all surpluses of income (or deficits) over time. The accumulated fund replaces capital in the balance sheet. Of course there are many types of not-for-profit organisations (e.g. clubs, charities), and each type of organisation may have its own peculiarities in the financial statements. Charities, for example, are subject to some quite specific accounting and legal requirements. However, if you have a good knowledge of a business balance sheet and know about accumulated funds, you're well on your way to understanding the balance sheet of a not-for-profit organisation.

That's it for the balance sheet. Now that you've learned the basics on both the income statement and balance sheet, the next chapter introduces the financial statements of companies, with Chapter 7 introducing a new financial statement called the cash flow statement.

 **brilliant** recap

- A balance lists the assets, liabilities and capital of a business.
- Assets and liabilities are categorised as non-current and non-current.
- A balance sheet will have two totals, which 'balance', i.e. equal each other.
- The capital of a business is an important component of the balance sheet.
- Balance sheets of partnerships show the capital for each partner.
- In not-for-profit organisations, the accumulated fund represents the surplus of income over time.

# CHAPTER 6

# Financial statements of limited companies

I n this chapter you'll learn about the income statement and balance sheet for limited companies. The techniques used in preparing the financial statements for companies are the same as those you learned in Chapter 5. However, there are quite a few accounting and legal rules which are relevant to the preparation of company accounts. These rules cover things that must be shown in the income statement and balance sheet, the layout of the financial statements and additional information which must be disclosed alongside the financial statements. Some of these accounting rules require the preparation of another financial statement called the cash flow statement, and you'll learn about this in Chapter 7. In this chapter, you'll see some of the more important rules and regulations relevant to the financial statements of companies. These come from two sources, company law and accounting standards, which are detailed later. First, you need to know more about the nature of limited companies.

## The nature of limited companies

A company differs from other business forms in that it is a separate legal entity from its owners. This means that a company is a separate legal 'person' and can take legal action in its own right – it can sue and be sued just like an individual. The owners of a company are called shareholders, who are the providers of capital to a company. Each shareholder buys (or agrees to buy) a share in the company. Once the shareholder has paid in full for their shares, they then have no further liability to repay any debts of the company. In other words, the liability of shareholders is *limited*.

Companies are usually either private or public. A private limited company (abbreviated as 'Ltd') cannot offer shares for sale to the public and is normally limited to a maximum of 50 shareholders. The vast majority of companies in the UK are private limited companies. Public limited companies (abbreviated as 'plc') can offer shares for sale to the public, usually through a stock exchange like the London Stock Exchange. Public companies are usually much larger than private companies and there is no limit on the number of shareholders. You'll learn more about the types of shares later.

## Company law

Limited companies, regardless of size or type, are regulated by legislation which is collectively referred to as the Companies Acts. These Acts lay down rules for many aspects of a limited company. For example, the Companies Acts specify the minimum number of shareholders required, the duties of company directors, and the frequency of general meetings of a company

The Companies Acts also contain a number of items relating to the format and content of financial statements. The Acts describe the minimum items which must be shown in financial statements. These minimum items depend on whether the company is small, medium or large. The size of the company is determined by a combination of the value of its assets, its turnover and the number of its employees, with the Acts defining what these values are.

All companies must make their financial statements available to the public. Publication is normally achieved by filing the required financial statements at a Registrar of Companies (this is Companies House in the UK). For example, a UK small company typically only has to publish a summarised balance sheet, whereas a large public company has to publish full details. In addition, the Companies Acts require two additional reports which you'll learn a little more about later: (1) a directors' report and, (2) an auditors' report.

Finally, the Companies Acts may also require a number of 'Notes to the Accounts'. You already know that a detailed capital account is a typical note to the balance sheet of a sole trader. Likewise in companies, these notes to the accounts give additional information to explain figures in the income statement or balance sheet. The notes include things such as details of directors' salaries, directors' shareholdings, numbers and salaries of staff, and details on non-current assets.

## Accounting standards

In addition to company law, accounting has a further set of rules and regulations called accounting standards. The vast majority of these accounting standards are relevant to limited companies.

Accounting standards fall into two main categories. First, they provide guidance on how to treat certain items in the financial statements. Second, they specify additional details to be provided on certain items which are contained in the income statement and balance sheet. There are quite a few accounting standards; many are complex and beyond the scope of this book. Until recently, many countries maintained their own unique set of accounting standards but, since 2004, the European Union has adopted the accounting standards set by the International Accounting Standards Board (IASB). These standards (known as International Financial Reporting Standards or IFRS) are now used in the preparation of the accounts of public companies in all European Union member states. Private companies also have the option to use IFRS. In the UK, accounting standards are set by the Accounting Standards Board (ASB) and these standards, known as Financial Reporting Standards (FRS), are applicable to private limited companies. It is likely, however, that by 2012 or 2013 all UK companies will adopt IFRS. At present a simplified version of IFRS used by public companies is available and it is likely to be adopted by the UK and Ireland for use in all companies.

The combination of accounting standards and companies legislation can make for some complex work in the preparation of company financial statements. You might be best getting help from an accountant, but at least by reading this chapter you'll be able to understand and interpret the financial statements of a company. Let's now look at the financial statements of private, and then public limited, companies.

# Financial statements of a private limited company

## Income statement

The income statement of a private limited company is not too different from that of a sole trader. Companies have some items of expenditure which are not seen in the accounts of a sole trader, so I'll explain some of these items before looking at an example.

First, directors' salaries and other remuneration are normal in a limited company. Directors are the persons responsible for the day-to-day running of a business. They may or may not be shareholders, i.e. owners of the company. Auditors' fees are another expense you'll see in company accounts. Auditors verify (i.e. audit) the financial statements of a company. An audit is required by company law, although smaller companies can be exempt. Sole traders and partnerships do not normally need an audit. Finally, the income statement will show a taxation charge. Companies pay corporation tax on their profits and this tax is shown as an expense in the income statement. However, as you'll see below, these expenses are not shown on the face of the income statement.

Let's look at an example now (see Figure 6.1). The layout of this income statement is in accordance with UK company law and UK accounting standards. You'll see it is actually called a profit and loss account, which is still used in smaller companies.

As you can see, the income statement is very brief. The first thing you'll notice is comparative figures, i.e. the previous year. This is normal and required by law. It's also quite useful to readers of the accounts as a picture of the performance year-on-year is possible (remember from Chapter 1 that an important function of accounting is to provide information). The income statement starts with a 'Turnover' figure, which represents the sales of the company. Cost of sales is the same for a sole trader, as is gross profit. Next, there is other operating income, which is income from items other than sales of products/services (e.g. interest, profit on the sale of assets or gains on foreign exchange transactions). Expenses are simply totalled under the heading of 'administrative expenses'. The term 'Profit on ordinary activities before interest and taxation' is used to describe what you know as net profit from Chapter 4. The taxation charge is shown and the retained profit after taxation.

Sample Company Ltd

Profit and Loss Account

For the year ended 31 December 2010

| | 2010<br>£000 | 2009<br>£000 |
|---|---|---|
| Turnover | 66,897 | 58,660 |
| Cost of sales | (53,778) | (47,345) |
| Other operating income | 4,070 | 250 |
| Operating profit | 17,189 | 11,565 |
| Administrative expenses | (9,302) | (9,154) |
| Profit on ordinary activities before interest and taxation | 7,887 | 2,411 |
| Taxation | (2,205) | (1,165) |
| Retained profit on ordinary activities after taxation | 5,682 | 1,246 |

Figure 6.1  Income statement of a private limited company

You are probably asking yourself whether the income statement of a company is that simple. The answer is yes, it is. The income statement (and balance sheet) is detailed further in what are called 'Notes on the Financial Statements'. These notes are required by company law or accounting standards. You don't need to know the full details of the law or standards, but examples of further information on the income statement given in the notes include:

● certain expenses like salaries, social insurance, and pension costs and payments to directors are detailed
● the average number of employees
● details of the taxation charged for the year.

That's it for the income statement. You'll see later in this chapter that the layout varies slightly for a public company.

## Balance sheet

Again, the balance sheet of a private limited company takes a similar format to that of a sole trader (have a look back at Figure 5.2). As with the income statement, there are a number of items found on a company balance sheet that are not found on the balance sheet of a sole trader. Figure 6.2 shows an example.

Sample Company Ltd

Balance Sheet

As at 31 December 2010

| | 2010 £000 | 2009 £000 |
|---|---|---|
| Fixed assets | | |
| Tangible fixed assets | 25,926 | 25,855 |
| | | |
| Current assets | | |
| Stocks | 8,814 | 11,750 |
| Debtors | 10,010 | 9,003 |
| Cash at bank | 36,884 | 26,628 |
| | 55,708 | 47,381 |
| | | |
| Current liabilities | | |
| Creditors: amounts falling due within one year | (10,818) | (8,666) |
| | | |
| Net current assets | 44,890 | 38,715 |
| | | |
| Total assets less current liabilities | 70,816 | 64,570 |
| | | |
| Creditors: amounts falling due after more than one year | (517) | |
| | | |
| Provisions for liabilities and charges | (2,936) | (3,178) |
| | | |
| NET ASSETS | 67,363 | 61,392 |
| | | |
| Capital and reserves | | |
| Ordinary share capital | 60,000 | 60,000 |
| Other reserves | 654 | 636 |
| Profit and loss account | 6,709 | 756 |
| | | |
| EQUITY SHAREHOLDERS' FUNDS | 67,363 | 61,392 |

Figure 6.2  Balance sheet of a private limited company

As was the case with the income statement, this balance sheet is not too detailed. It is also quite like the sole trader balance sheet you already know. The top portion of the balance sheet shows the fixed assets. 'Fixed assets' is a term still used in private company accounts and is the same as non-current assets. Below this, you can see current assets and current liabilities. The term 'Creditors: amounts falling due within one year' is a term in company law which describes all trade creditors, accruals and other amounts due within one year. Just below this, you can see another new term 'Creditors: amounts falling due after more than one year'. This term again comes from company law and describes amounts owed after more than one year. You might see the term 'long-term liabilities' used in a similar way in sole trader accounts. Normally, if for example a loan is due over five years, the amount shown within one year is included in the 'Creditors: amounts falling due within one year' heading, with the balance included under the 'after more than one year heading'. Below this again is a new heading: 'Provisions for liabilities and charges'. Accounting standards require companies to recognise probable future liabilities in the accounts, where these liabilities arise from past events. For example, a car manufacturer will most likely have to repair some cars under warranty (they sold the cars in the past), so a provision for future warranties is created. Another example would be a provision for future redundancy payments. These provisions are created by reducing the profits in a particular year – in effect an expense in the income statement. Finally, the bottom portion of the balance sheet is termed 'Capital and reserves'. Under this heading you can see share capital, other reserves and the profit and loss account. The latter is the accumulated profits over time. Share capital and reserves are explained below.

 **brilliant** definition

Share capital is money obtained by a company from issuing shares to investors. Authorised share capital is the maximum amount of share capital a company can issue, whereas issued share capital refers to the amount of share capital issued.

The maximum amount of shares any company issues, i.e. the authorised capital, is defined in a document called the 'Memorandum and Articles of Association'. This is a legal document drawn up when a company is formed. This document can of course be changed at a later date. A company's share capital may consist of either ordinary shares or preference shares.

 **brilliant** definition

An ordinary share (in the US, a common stock) gives the holder partial ownership of a company. Holders of ordinary shares are entitled to voting rights in proportion to their holding and may receive a dividend. A

**preference share** is a share which pays a regular and fixed return. Preference shareholders have a claim on the profits of a company before ordinary shareholders and normally preference shares do not carry any voting rights. All shares have a nominal value, which is often £1.

**brilliant** definition

A **dividend** is a portion of profits paid to shareholders. It is not shown as an expense in the income statement, rather in a note to the accounts. There is no obligation on a company to pay a dividend.

Holders of ordinary shares may receive a dividend and preference shareholders are typically guaranteed one. On the other hand, ordinary shareholders have some control over a company in that they can vote at the annual general meeting – a meeting which must be held under company law to do things like approve the accounts and appoint directors. Many larger companies have a far greater proportion of ordinary shareholders.

You're probably thinking this is all quite complex. In a typical, small, family run company though, there may be two shareholders (the husband and wife perhaps) and that's it. In larger private and public companies there may be many shareholders and these will expect a dividend for risking their investment in shares in the company.

**brilliant** definition

A **reserve** is an amount of money put aside from profits to provide for items such as future expansion, acquisitions, or guarding against future liabilities.

In Figure 6.2, the general reserve is most likely a 'rainy' day fund, where the company does not yet have a specific purpose for these funds. However, by setting a portion of profits aside, less is available for dividends. Many larger companies have such a reserve.

Finally, the bottom total of the balance sheet in Figure 6.2 is termed 'Equity shareholders' funds'. The term equity is defined as follows.

 **brilliant definition**

In accounting, **equity** refers to the ownership interest in a company in the form of ordinary or preference shares.

As shareholders are the owners of a company, they also 'own' the profits, so accumulated profit is regarded as part of equity. Reserves, such as the general reserve in Figure 6.2 are also equity as these have been set aside from previous profits. A company may also have debt finance (e.g. loans) and you'll learn about this when we look at public companies later below.

Again, as with the income statement/profit and loss account shown in Figure 6.1, more detail on a company balance sheet is provided in the notes to the accounts. For example, a detailed breakdown of tangible fixed assets is required. This note shows each class of asset (e.g. buildings, motors and so on), as well as the cost, accumulated depreciation, book value and additions/disposals by each class. Further detail on the make-up of debtors, creditors and any tax liability is also required as is detail of the share capital (e.g. details of the value of each share or any shares issued during the year).

As you can see in Figure 6.2, the accounting equation applies in a company balance sheet in the same way as a sole trader or partnership. While accounting in limited companies may mean lot of rules and regulations have to be complied with, you now know that the main financial statements are not all that different. Now let's look at the income statement and balance sheet of public limited companies.

## Financial statements of a public limited company

You'll now learn about the basic content and layout of the financial statements of a public limited company. These companies can be very large and complex, but nonetheless produce income statements and balance sheets which are not too dissimilar to what you know about private companies. I'll give you the basics here, but bear in mind that the variety of companies out there is vast and you may find some items in public company accounts that I don't cover here.

## Income statement

As mentioned earlier in this chapter, the financial statements of public limited companies are regulated by International Financial Reporting Standards (IFRS). Since January 2005, all public companies throughout the European Union must use IFRS. The basics of the income statement (and balance sheet) are similar to what you know about private companies. There are a few differences in the wording used and in the layout. Figure 6.3 shows a sample of an income statement according to IFRS.

Sample plc
Income statement
For the year ended 30 June 2010

| | £m |
|---|---|
| Revenue | 20,992 |
| Cost of sales | (14,715) |
| Gross profit | 6,277 |
| Operating costs | (4,191) |
| Operating profit | 2,086 |
| Finance costs | (416) |
| Finance revenue | 170 |
| Share of associates' profit | 64 |
| Profit before tax | 1,904 |
| Income tax expense | (466) |
| Profit for the financial year | 1,438 |
| Attributable to: | |
| Equity shareholders | 1,430 |
| Minority interests | 8 |

Figure 6.3 Income statement of a public limited company

The first thing you'll notice is that the term 'Income statement' is used, not profit and loss account. Again, the income statement is brief with not too much detail, but I'll explain some items. Revenue is simply the revenue generated from the operations of the company, i.e. turnover or sales. Cost of sales is the same for a sole trader or private limited company, as is gross profit. Expenses are simply totalled under the heading of 'operating costs'. Finance costs and finance revenues are expenses such as interest paid and received. As in a private company, the 'Income tax expense' amount refers to the taxation payable on the profits of the company.

There are a number of new items, which you are likely to see quite often in large public companies. Share of associates profit is something which is normally in a group income statement, i.e. the combined income statement of a group of companies (most large public companies are groups of companies).

### brilliant definition

An **associate company** within a group of companies is one where 20–50% of the ordinary shares are owned by the parent company. More than 50% ownership of a company means a company is a **subsidiary company** within a group, and such a company is assumed to be controlled or owned by the parent. The part of a subsidiary company not owned by a group is called the **minority (or non-controlling) interest**.

The above definition is a very brief summary of what happens in many public companies which are a large group of companies. When the financial statements of a group of companies are prepared, it is assumed that all subsidiary companies are 100% owned. This makes the adding together of income and expenses a lot easier. Then, the accounts are adjusted to show the portion of profit (in the income statement) and ownership (in the balance sheet) which are owned by minority interests. For associate companies (20–50% ownership), as majority ownership does not occur; only a portion of the profits is shown in the income statement of the parent with no ownership in the balance sheet. Looking at Figure 6.3, you'll see how the last two items show the amount of the profit which is attributable to the group and to minority interests – these are the last two items. You can also see an item 'share of associates' profits', which is the portion of profit from associated companies which belongs to the group of companies (i.e. Sample plc).

As you can see, the level of detail in the income statement of a public limited company is quite similar to that you have seen above for private companies. Again, notes to the income statement will provide more detail. With IFRS, many more notes are typically required than with smaller private companies. These are beyond the scope of this book but suffice it to say that the notes required are more detailed than those typically seen in the accounts of a private limited company. But, if you want to know more, visit the website of any public company you know and have a look under the 'Investor Relations' section, where you will find lots more details in the company's annual report.

## Balance sheet

The balance sheet of a public company is also subject to IFRS. In Figure 6.4 you can see the balance sheet of Sample plc. I'll explain some of the items but, as with the income statement (above), more detailed information will be given in notes to the balance sheet. You might also notice the layout is a little different; more on this later.

## Assets

The assets shown on a public company balance sheet are split as non-current and current – the term fixed assets is not used for public companies as IFRS adopts the term 'non-current'. Looking first at non-current assets, you will see some new terms, which I'll now explain.

## Property, plant and equipment

IFRS requires a public company to show one figure for all its physical assets and this is called 'property, plant and equipment'. More detail is given in a note to the accounts, which like in a private company shows the opening balance for each class of asset, additions, disposals and deprecation.

## Intangible assets

This is a new term. Non-current (or fixed) assets can be either tangible assets – something we can see and touch – or intangible assets, which are assets that are not physical in nature but can deliver future economic benefits. The most common intangible asset is goodwill.

Sample plc
Balance Sheet
As at 30 June 2010

|  | £m |
|---|---|
| **ASSETS** | |
| **Non-current assets** | |
| Plant, property and equipment | 8,226 |
| Intangible assets | 3,692 |
| Investments in associates | 1,112 |
|  | 13,030 |
| **Current assets** | |
| Inventories | 2,226 |
| Trade receivables | 3,199 |
| Cash and cash equivalents | 1,333 |
|  | 6,758 |
|  | |
| **Total assets** | 19,788 |
|  | |
| **EQUITY** | |
| Equity share capital | 187 |
| Preference shares | 1 |
| Share premium | 2,420 |
| Retained income | 5,346 |
|  | 7,954 |
| Minority interest | 66 |
| Total equity | 8,020 |
|  | |
| **LIABILITIES** | |
| **Non-current liabilities** | |
| Loans and borrowings | 5,928 |
| Deferred income tax | 1,312 |
| Trade and other payments | 141 |
| Provisions for liabilities | 406 |
|  | 7,787 |
| **Current liabilities** | |
| Trade and other payments | 2,956 |
| Current income tax | 244 |
| Loans and borrowings | 570 |
| Other liabilities | 211 |
|  | 3,981 |
|  | |
| **Total equity and liabilities** | 19,788 |

Figure 6.4  Balance sheet of a public limited company

 **brilliant** definition

Goodwill occurs when one business buys another. It is the amount of money over and above the book value of the net assets of a firm that a buyer is willing to pay, for example for reputation, know-how or a strong customer following.

Thinking back to Chapter 3, here's an example of how goodwill is accounted for in the general ledger.

 **example**

Assume £7.5m is paid for a business which has net assets (i.e. assets less liabilities) totalling £6m. £1.5m over the odds is paid because the business has built up a good reputation over the years and has a strong customer base. Assuming the purchase price of £7.5m is paid in cash, the ledger entries would be:

|                                         | £     |
| --------------------------------------- | ----- |
| Debit: Plant, property and equipment    | 6.0m  |
| Debit: Goodwill                         | 1.5m  |
| Credit: Bank                            | 7.5m  |

The balance sheet after the purchase of the new business in the example above will show goodwill as an intangible asset with a value of £1.5m; just like the sample balance sheet in Figure 6.4. Only *purchased* goodwill (i.e. the £1.5m in the example above) can be included in a balance sheet. It is not permitted under accounting regulations to 'value' the goodwill of a business and place it on a balance sheet.

## Investments in associates

You already know what an associate company is, as you have seen this term above while looking at the income statement of public companies. A large public company will normally invest in, or buy, other companies as part of its longer-term view. Therefore, an investment in an associate company is shown as a non-current asset as it is expected to be held for more than one year (see Figure 6.4 above, where the amount is £1,112m). If the investment is in a subsidiary company (50% or greater ownership), the assets and liabilities are added to the assets and liabilities of the parent in the balance sheet. Then in a similar process to that explained for the income statement above, the minority interest portion is removed. I'll explain this in a little more detail shortly.

## Current assets

Looking at the current assets of Sample plc in Figure 6.4, these are quite similar to those we have seen in a sole trader's balance sheet (look back at Figure 5.2 and Figure 5.4). One key element about the terms used here is that they are specified by IFRS. For example, *only* the terms 'inventories' and 'receivables' are used in a public company, whereas in a sole trader or private company you could use 'stocks' or 'debtors' respectively. There is also a new term 'cash and cash equivalents'. This simply refers to cash held at the bank and other short-term deposits; what you have learned as the 'bank' figure previously.

## Equity

You already know what ordinary shares, preference shares and retained earnings are from earlier in this chapter. Note that IFRS uses the term 'retained earnings' to describe the accumulated profit and loss account you've seen in Figure 6.2.

## Share premium

Shares are issued at what is called a nominal (or par) value. This might be £1, for example. Investors may be willing to pay a lot more than this price as they take account of both the past and future performance of the company. In accounting, shares are always shown in the balance sheet at nominal value. Any additional amount received when shares are sold is shown as a share premium. For example, in Sample plc, the share premium is £2,420m, which is quite a bit more than the £188m in equity and preference shares. It is quite normal to see a large share premium in the balance sheet of a successful public company as shareholders are willing to pay over the odds in the hope of obtaining a good return in the longer term.

## Minority interest

The minority (or non-controlling) interest shown in the balance sheet is to reflect the assets which do not belong to Sample plc. As mentioned earlier, when a group of companies prepare accounts, all assets are assumed 100% owned even if they are not. This makes adding together the accounts of multiple companies a lot easier. Then any minority interest is shown separately, i.e. the £66m in Figure 6.4. Note that IFRS actually uses the term non-controlling interest rather than minority interest, but this latter term is still very commonly used.

## Liabilities

Liabilities are split between non-current and current, as for assets. As you can see in the balance sheet of Sample plc, trade payables and bank loans are shown and are divided between non-current and current depending on when they are due for payment – that is, within one year or after one year. Note that the term 'trade payables' is used by IFRS in preference to 'creditors'. There are some other items which you need a little more detail on, as you'll quite often see these in the balance sheet of a public company.

## Deferred income tax

Deferred income tax is tax for which payment has been deferred until later. It results from differences in how profits are calculated for taxation purposes compared to accounting. For example, it may be possible to reduce profits for taxation purposes by the full amount invested in new equipment. This means that the tax liability is greatly reduced. A simple example to help you understand this is shown below.

 **example**

Assume a company buys an asset for £1,000 and depreciates it over five years on a straight line basis. For taxation purposes, the same asset can be depreciated by 25% on a reducing balance basis. Taxation on profits is 20%. Now take a look at the numbers below.

| Year end | Year 1 | Year 2 | Year 3 | Year 4 |
| --- | --- | --- | --- | --- |
| Accounting value of asset | 800 | 600 | 400 | 200 |
| Tax value of asset | 750 | 563 | 422 | 316 |
| Temporary difference | 50 | 37 | (22) | (116) |
| Deferred liability/(asset) at 20% | 10 | 7 | (4) | (23) |

In the above example, in years 1 and 2, the tax depreciation is greater than the accounting depreciation, so there will be additional tax to be paid in the future which is recognised as a liability. In years 3 and 4, the opposite is the case.

## Provisions for liabilities

According to IFRS, a provision is a liability of uncertain timing or amount. For example, if a company gives a warranty on its products it is likely at some time to have to repair or replace products under the warranty. The exact timing and amount of any warranty claims are not certain, but nonetheless a provision should be made in the accounts. Making such a provision is applying the prudence concept.

## Current income tax

The current liability for income tax shown on the balance sheet of Sample plc is simply the amount of tax owed to the taxation authorities. As taxation is calculated based on profits at the accounting year end, a liability will exist in the balance sheet until it is paid.

## The annual report

If you look at the website of a public company you'll typically find the company's annual report under an 'Investor Relations' or 'Investor Centre' link. So before we continue, why not go to the website of any public company you like (or dislike!) and see if you can find its most recent annual report.

An annual report of a company is a document presented to shareholders at the Annual General Meeting (AGM) and some of its contents is required by company law. The precise contents of an annual report vary from company to company, but there are a number of common items which I'll outline below. One of the most important (and required) features is the financial statements, which you already know about.

## Business review

The annual report generally contains a section which reviews the operations of the company. For example, if you look at the 2009 annual report for Tesco plc (http://www.tescoplc.com), a review of operations is given on the following operating sections: international, core UK, non-food and retailing services. The business review gives information on things like market conditions, sales growth, branding and plans for the future.

## Financial review

Many annual reports give a one- or two-page summary of the main financial highlights for the year. A financial review might include summary data on revenue, profits, major costs, acquisitions and capital expenditure. Charts are often used to summarise data and make it more understandable to the general public.

## Corporate governance

Corporate governance is the set of processes, customs, policies, laws and institutions affecting the way a company is directed, administered or controlled. It also includes the relationships among the many stakeholders involved and the goals for which the corporation is governed.

 **brilliant** definition

A **stakeholder** is a party who affects, or can be affected by, a company's actions. Stakeholders include managers, employees, suppliers, customers, shareholders and the local community.

A report on corporate governance includes items such as details of the board of directors and their duties, directors' shareholdings, environmental policy, fairness to employees and political donations.

## Auditors' report

Under company law, the financial statements of a company must be audited (checked and verified) by an independent external auditor. An audit is an independent assessment of the fairness of the way a company's financial statements are presented by its management. It is performed by a competent, independent and objective person or persons, known as auditors, who then issue a report on the results of the audit. The auditors' report states whether or not the financial statements of the company are a fair representation of the underlying books of account. Smaller companies may claim what is known as an audit exemption, if permitted under company law. This does not, however, remove the need to produce financial statements.

To summarise, while the financial statements are a large part of an annual report, it includes other items. Most public companies now publish their annual report on the company's website.

 **brilliant** recap

- In general terms, company financial statements are similar to any other.
- There are some new items, including expenditure, assets and liabilities that are unique to companies.
- There are some new terms used to describe some assets and liabilities. These terms are defined by company law and accounting standards.
- The capital of a company consists of share capital and retained profits.
- The annual report of a company includes the financial statements and some other reports required by law. It also includes some useful features which are of interest to investors.

# CHAPTER 7

# Cash flow
# statements

In God we trust, all others pay cash.

*Anonymous*

n Chapter 2, you've learned that goods are bought and sold on credit. Payment is made or received at some point in the future, and cash is received or paid at this point. You'll learn in Chapter 9 that a business should plan its cash requirements, but from what you know at this point you might have noticed that the income statement and balance sheet, while including some cash, also include many items which are not cash per se. For example, trade receivables represent the amount of money owed from customers and are current assets. It is not the amount of cash received from customers during a year, rather the amount to be received in the future. In the income statement, too, there are a number of items which are not cash, for example depreciation, accrual and prepayments. Even the sales figure in the income statement does not normally equate to the amount of cash received from customers during a year.

As neither the income statement nor balance sheet actually tells us a great deal about the cash flowing into and out of a business, a further financial statement can be prepared. This is called simply the 'cash flow statement'. According to accounting regulations, only limited companies need prepare cash flow statements, with an exemption for small companies. The current definition of a small company as per UK company law is where at least two of the following conditions are met:

- Turnover must be £5.6m or less.
- The balance sheet total must be £2.8m or less.
- The average number of employees is 50 or less.

These conditions change from time to time, so ask your accountant or check on www.companieshouse.gov.uk.

This chapter shows you how to prepare a cash flow statement and what the accounting regulations require. It is unlikely you'll ever prepare a cash flow statement yourself, as normally accountants or auditors do this. Nonetheless, understanding the cash flow statement is useful as it identifies the sources and uses of cash in a business and might be useful to assess the ability of a business to generate cash.

Why is cash so important to a business? Simply, a business needs cash to be able to pay wages, suppliers, loans and so on. If sufficient cash is not available a business will stall. The term insolvency, which you may know from news reports, means that a business cannot pay its debts as they fall due, and one major reason for this is the inability to generate enough cash. Later in Chapter 10, you'll learn more about how to notice indicators of cash flow problems in the balance sheet.

## Sources and uses of cash

The basic purpose of a cash flow statement is to show where a business generated cash and what cash was used for. Have a look at Table 7.1, which identifies the main sources and uses of cash for a typical business.

|   | Cash sources | Cash uses |
|---|---|---|
| 1 | Profits | Losses |
| 2 | Sale of assets | Purchases of assets |
| 3 | Selling stocks (inventory) | Buying stocks (inventory) |
| 4 | Getting paid by customers | Giving credit to customers |
| 5 | Share capital issued | Dividends |
| 6 | Loans received | Loans repaid |
| 7 | Getting credit from suppliers | Paying suppliers |

Table 7.1 Typical sources and uses of cash

I'll explain each briefly.

1 Profits bring cash into the business, losses the opposite. Profit is not necessarily 100% cash, but we'll deal with this shortly.

2 A sale of a non-current asset brings in cash, while a purchase requires cash to be paid out.

3 If stock is sold, or in other words, the amount of stock held decreases, this means that in the normal course of business it is being sold and turned into cash. If the amount of stock increases, cash is effectively tied up.

4 If customers pay, or in other words receivables decrease, this means your customers have paid you cash. The opposite applies if receivables increase, as cash is tied up until payment arrives.

5 Issuing new shares for cash is a source of cash for a company. Dividends paid to shareholders are a use of cash.

6 If a company raises finance through a bank loan, this is a source of cash. Likewise, cash can be used to reduce or repay loans and interest on loans.

7 If you get credit from suppliers, or in other words payables increase, cash is retained in the business rather than paid to suppliers. A decrease means suppliers have been paid using cash.

A cash flow statement explains the increase or decrease in cash over the financial year. Therefore, starting with the cash balance at the start of the year, sources of cash are added and uses of cash subtracted to give the closing cash balance. Put another way, the cash flow statement should be able to explain the difference in the cash balances on the balance sheet between one year and the previous year.

 **brilliant** definition

A **cash flow statement** shows the changes in the cash balance of a business and analyses the sources and uses of cash.

## Constructing the cash flow statement

There are two ways to prepare a cash flow statement. First, the *direct method* uses the exact cash flows (in and out) of a business. This might sound easy, but remember how the double entry accounting system works. All transactions are recorded according to the accruals concept (as explained in Chapter 1) and not when cash is paid. Therefore, rather than keep a second set of 'cash' records, most businesses use an *indirect method*. This means using the existing financial statements to indirectly derive the cash flows. Let's use a simple example to see how this works. Below are summarised balance sheets of a company for two years.

| Balance sheet as at 31 July | 2009 £m | 2010 £m |
|---|---|---|
| Non-current assets at cost | 160 | 230 |
| Accumulated depreciation | (60) | (90) |
| | 100 | 140 |
| Inventory | 29 | 54 |
| Bank and cash | 7 | 22 |
| | 136 | 216 |
| | | |
| Equity and liabilities | | |
| Share capital | 55 | 71 |
| Share premium account | 9 | 13 |
| Retained profits | 45 | 95 |
| Payables | 27 | 37 |
| | 136 | 216 |

Look closely at each item on these balance sheets and you'll see what has happened from 2009 to 2010:

- The cost of fixed assets went up by £70m, which suggests a purchase of assets.
- The depreciation on assets was £30m (£90m–£60m) in 2010.
- Inventory went up by £25m, tying up cash.
- The bank (i.e. cash) balance increased by £15m.
- Share capital increased by £16m, suggesting shares were issued for cash. Share premium increased by £4m (see Chapter 6), too, meaning the total cash from the share issue was £20m.

● Retained profits went up by £50m, meaning the profit for 2010 was £50m. Some of this profit figure represents cash flows.

Now we can prepare a simple cash flow statement, showing our sources and uses of cash.

**Cash flow statement for the year ended 31 July 2010**

|  | £m |
|---|---|
| Cash inflows: | |
| Profit for the year (95 − 45) | 50 |
| Depreciation charges (90 − 60) | 30 |
| Funds generated from trading | 80 |
| Issue of shares (incl. share premium) | 20 |
| Increase in payables | 10 |
|  | 110 |
| Cash outflows: | |
| Purchases of fixed assets | (70) |
| Increase in stock | (25) |
|  | (95) |
| Increase in cash | 15 |

I'll explain some of the figures in more detail.

● The profit is adjusted by depreciation by adding it back. The profit for the year (£50m) is after depreciation and, as depreciation is not a cash flow (it's an accounting adjustment) it is added back to work out the amount of cash received from trading.

● Payables have increased by £10m, or effectively generated a cash inflow of £10m as this cash has not been paid out to suppliers or other creditors.

● Stocks have increase by £25m, which effectively means this cash is tied up, or is an outflow.

The example above shows the basics of how to prepare a cash flow statement from the balance sheet and/or income statement. Before you learn what accounting standards say, let's examine in more detail how to derive the cash element of profit, which is called 'cash flow from operating activities'. When calculating the cash flow from operating activities, you begin with the profit per the income statement and adjust for the effects of certain items, which are now outlined.

## The effect of depreciation on cash flow

As you have seen above, depreciation needs to be added back to profit because (1) the profit per the income statement is after any depreciation charge and (2) depreciation is not a cash flow. You learned about depreciation in Chapter 4 (see p. 77), and about the profit or loss arising when an asset is sold. Remember that a loss on the sale of an asset means additional depreciation has been charged, so this too would have to be added back to profit if a cash flow statement is being prepared. The reverse applies when a profit on the sale of an asset occurs, i.e. the profit on the sale is deducted from profit for the purposes of the cash flow statement.

## The effect of inventories on cash flow

At the end of a financial year, most companies will have inventories (stocks of raw materials or finished goods). Inventories, as you know, are a current asset and the value of inventory also reduces the cost of sales in the income statement. Buying inventory does require cash, which means cash flows out of the business. In the cash flow statement, it is assumed all inventory is paid for (see payables later). Thus, if its value increases, cash flows out of the business, meaning that the cash flow is less than profit. The reverse applies if inventory value decreases.

## The effect of receivables on cash flow

Most sales are on credit, which means cash flow will occur at some future date after the date of sale. Have a look at the brilliant example below.

## brilliant example

Let's assume at the beginning of a year your business is owed £25,000 from customers. Your sales are £120,000, expenses £70,000, thus giving a profit of £50,000. Assuming no other adjustments to profit and all customers have paid you, the cash flow at the end of the year would be £75,000 (£50,000 + £25,000). Now suppose you are owed £30,000 by customers at the end of the year. The cash flows would now be the £75,000 as before, but less £30,000 still owed, making it £45,000. A quicker way to work this out is to look at the increase or decrease in the amounts owed (receivables). In this example, the total amount owed increases by £5,000, which is cash tied up or, in other words, cash flows out. So, an increase in receivables is a cash outflow and will reduce the cash from operating activities, while a decrease will increase it. In this example, the total cash flows are £45,000, which is £50,000 from profit less the increase in receivables of £5,000.

# The effect of payables on cash flow

Probably the best way to think of the effect of changes in amounts owed (payables) is to consider them as being the opposite of receivables. In other words, an increase in payables is equivalent to a cash inflow since we are effectively getting cash from suppliers by not paying them. A decrease in payables is the opposite and is equivalent to a cash outflow.

The effects of inventory, receivables and payables on cash flows are picked up from the balance sheet. As in the earlier example, balance sheets for two consecutive years are needed to identify these increases or decreases in each. The cash flow statements we have looked at thus far are not the same as what companies actually prepare. The next section explains what the accounting regulations require. However, the basic principle stands: a cash flow statement simply shows the cash inflows (sources of cash) and outflows (uses of cash) for a period of time and these cash flows are derived from the income statement and balance sheet.

# The cash flow statement per accounting standards

International Accounting Standard 7 (IAS7) gives detail on the classifications of cash inflows and outflows to be used when preparing a cash flow statement. Thus far I have not classified cash sources or uses in any way. IAS7 specifies three classifications of cash flows:

1 cash flows from operating activities

2 cash flows from financing activities

3 cash flows from investing activities.

Figure 7.1 below shows an example cash flow statement of a public limited company based on IAS7.

**Cash Flow Statement of BBB plc for the year ended 31/12/2010**

| | | £m |
|---|---|---|
| *Cash flows from operating activities* | | |
| Cash generated by operations | (Note 1) | 4,099 |
| Interest paid | | (410) |
| Taxation paid | | (346) |
| Net cash from operating activities | | 3,343 |
| | | |
| *Cash flows from investing activities* | | |
| Acquisition of subsidiary companies | | (169) |
| Purchase of plant, property and equipment | | (3,442) |
| Proceeds from sales of plant, property and equipment | | 1,056 |
| Dividends received | | 216 |
| Increase in short term investments | | (615) |
| | | (2,954) |
| | | |
| *Cash flows from financing activities* | | |
| Proceeds from issue of shares | | 154 |
| Increase in borrowings | | 9.333 |
| Borrowings repaid | | (7,593) |
| Dividends paid | | (1,482) |
| | | 412 |
| | | |
| Net increase/(decrease) in cash | | 801 |
| Cash at beginning of year | | 987 |
| Cash at the end of year | | 1,788 |
| | | |
| Note 1 | | |
| | | |
| Profit before tax | | 2,791 |
| Depreciation | | 992 |
| Profit on sale of assets | | (188) |
| Increase in inventories | | (276) |
| Increase in receivables | | (71) |
| Increase in payables | | 851 |
| Cash generated by operations | | 4,099 |

Figure 7.1 Sample cash flow statement according to IAS7

As you can see, the cash flows are simply grouped according to the mentioned classifications. Don't worry about the detail of each cash flow; it is the classifications that are important. Why these three classifications? The amount of cash flows arising from operating activities is obviously a key indicator of the performance of the operations of a business. Reporting cash from operations shows whether a company has enough cash to pay loans, dividends and make investments. A separate classification for cash from investing activities is useful as this represents investment in possible future sources of cash, e.g. new non-current assets or acquiring subsidiaries. Finally, cash flows from financing help providers of finance assess the ability to take additional claims on cash (e.g. the ability to repay loans). You can also see in Figure 7.1 how Note 1 explains how the 'cash generated from operations' figure is calculated. Such a note is required by IAS7 to explain how the cash element of profit is worked out.

With the classifications of cash flows under IAS7, users of financial statements have the ability to assess the ability of a company to generate cash. Many decisions taken by investors are based on the ability of a company to generate cash flows. This is something which is not immediately possible to glean from the income statement and balance sheet.

## Benefits and drawbacks of the cash flow statement

In comparison to the income statement and balance sheet, you may find the cash flow statement easy to understand. Cash is cash; it is not subjective in any way. This is the greatest advantage of a cash flow statement. For example, when comparing two companies (which you'll learn about in Chapter 10) accounting techniques like depreciation may be inconsistent: maybe one company uses 10% straight line, whereas the other uses 20% reducing balance on the same class of assets. Using the cash flow statement to see cash invested in new assets, the figures are more comparable. A further advantage is that, in reality, the survival of a company depends on its ability to generate cash and have it available as needed. Lenders, suppliers and shareholders will use the cash flow statement to see if adequate cash is being generated to pay loans, payables and dividends.

There are drawbacks of cash flow statements, too. One is that IAS7 does allow flexibility in the classification of cash flows. For example, one company might classify dividends paid as an operating cash flow, while another might classify it as a financing cash flow. Another drawback is that cash flows can be erratic at times, making comparisons year-on-year difficult. For instance, there may be a lot of investing cash flows in one year and none for several years after.

As noted earlier in this chapter, it is unlikely that you will ever have to prepare a cash flow statement yourself. It is good though to understand the nature of the cash flow statement as cash is crucial to the survival of a business. At least now you have a basic understanding which should be sufficient to allow you to interpret a cash flow statement of any business.

 **brilliant** recap

- Companies must prepare a cash flow statement.
- A cash flow statement shows the sources and uses of cash.
- Cash flow is not the same as profit, but is extremely important for the survival of a business.
- A cash flow statement is often prepared indirectly from the income statement and balance sheet.
- IAS7 provides classifications for cash flows on the cash flow statement.

**PART 3**

# Using accounting to help manage a business

**CHAPTER 8**

# Understanding costs

The cost of freedom is high, but Americans have always paid it.

*John F. Kennedy*

In general language, the word 'cost' means many things. The above quote from John F. Kennedy suggests there is a price for freedom. But what is that price is another question. In accounting, the term cost is a little more concrete in that it will have measurable value, i.e. it has a monetary value.

In this chapter you'll learn some concepts from the management accounting branch of accounting. This branch of accounting is less concerned with the preparation of financial statements and more with providing information to make business decisions. Businesses make decisions on things like product prices, which customer to sell to, etc. on a daily basis. These decisions require a good understanding of the nature of the business, and its underlying costs. For example, in my book *Bookkeeping and Accounting for Entrepreneurs*, I cite the example of a business which appeared on the BBC's *Dragon's Den*. The business was selling Asian ready-meals to the large multiples like Morrison and Sainsbury. The Dragons were very interested, but after a bit of tough questioning, it turned out that the products were being sold at a loss. This was due in part to a lack of knowledge of the underlying costs. Quite a big mistake I think you'll agree. In the following sections you'll learn about how costs behave and what costs are relevant to decisions. This will help you appreciate the cost structures of a business and its product costs.

One of the fundamental aspects of management accounting is to understand and classify costs of a business. But first, what do we mean by cost?

**brilliant** definition

Cost is a monetary measure of resources sacrificed or forgone to achieve an objective.

What this definition shows is that you need to understand that cost means a little more than paying money out. For example, your business might choose to work overtime for a special request from customer A. The cost of overtime can be readily identified. But what if you lost an order from customer B because you had no time to deal with them? Let's now learn how costs are grouped in ways that makes cost information more useful.

## Classifying costs

In general, costs are classified in three main ways:

1  by how they behave when output increases or decreases,
2  by how they relate to the product or service provided, and
3  how relevant they are to decision making.

## Costs by behaviour

One way to classify costs is according to their behaviour when the level of business activity changes. As you might guess, a fixed cost is one which does not change, no matter what the business output.

 **brilliant** definition

A fixed cost remains stable within a relevant range of business activity.

For example, even if a business sells absolutely nothing, there will still be insurance costs. But, as business activity increases, the fixed cost for each 'unit' of output falls – a unit is the product sold or service provided. For example, if fixed costs are £50,000 and 10,000 units of a product are sold, then the fixed cost for each item is £5. If 20,000 units are sold the fixed cost per unit would be only £2.50. A key point in the definition above is that fixed costs can and do change, but this usually only happens when output increases beyond current activity levels. For example, salaries of customer service staff will be fixed regardless of sales levels. However, if sales were to increase dramatically, more staff might be needed and this increases costs. Other typical examples of fixed costs are things like managers' salaries, rent and insurance.

### brilliant definition

A **variable cost** increases in line with business activity.

Variable costs increase or decrease in line with change in business activity. For example, if a business manufactures a product, the materials required for the product are a variable cost. The more produced, the greater the total material cost. If nothing is produced, the material cost would be nil.

The classification of costs as fixed or variable is not written in stone. Some costs may be both fixed and variable – for example, a utility bill (e.g. water, electricity) typically has a small fixed charge and a variable charge based on consumption. It is also often difficult to decide what is fixed or variable and businesses will classify things differently.

## Cost classifications for products or services

Costs of making a product or delivering a service are usually classified according to whether they are direct or indirect.

### brilliant definition

A **direct cost** can be specifically identified to a particular product or service.
An **indirect cost** cannot be specifically attributed to products or services.

Direct costs normally consist of material and labour cost. In the case of direct material cost, this consists of all materials physically consumed by a product or service For example, a Dell notebook computer will have various electronic components for which the costs can be easily identified. Direct labour means the labour cost of all people engaged physically in the product or service. For example, production line workers at a Honda factory or the kitchen staff in a restaurant.

Indirect costs, or overheads as they are commonly known, are costs which cannot be traced specifically to a product or service. For example, an indirect labour cost might be the costs of having maintenance staff on a production line. The maintenance crew wages and any spare or replacement parts used are maintenance costs, but these cannot normally be traced to any one particular product or service. Another example is salaries of managers and other administration staff. It is normal to sub-classify overhead costs into manufacturing, selling or administrative.

Regardless of whether a cost is direct or indirect, it needs to be included in the cost of the product or service. If you don't do this, then you might be selling at a loss. I'll return to this important point below.

## Relevant costs for business decisions

Some costs are relevant to business decisions, some are not. This in fact is the most basic way to classify costs when referring to costs needed to help make decisions.

 **brilliant** definition

A **relevant cost** is a future cost that will change as a result of a decision. An **irrelevant cost** is one which is not affected by a decision.

Consider a simple business trip which you can make by car or train. Ask yourself what are the costs of each option and jot them down below. Assume the train journey starts at the station, so you ignore the costs of getting to the station.

| Trip by car | Trip by train |
| --- | --- |
| | |

_____

_____

_____

_____

_____

_____

If your list contains costs for the trip by car like insurance and motor tax, you're wrong. These costs are incurred even if the trip was not taken, so to compare like with like, you have to compare only the relevant costs. The relevant costs for the trip by car are fuel and wear and tear (see Depreciation, p. 77), and the relevant cost for the train journey is simply the ticket price. Here's a more realistic example.

## brilliant example

A business gets a request from a customer to make and deliver a special order. The material cost is £100 and these materials are in stock and have no other use. The cost of labour and delivery is £200 and the customer is prepared to pay £250. Should the business accept this order?

On the face of it the answer is no. This is because the costs are £300 (£100 materials + £200 other costs) versus only £250 income, so a loss of £50 would be made. This is not correct however. This is because the material cost of £100 has already been incurred and so is not relevant to the decision – it will not change whether the order is accepted or not. Therefore, a profit of £50 (£250 – £200) is made by accepting this customer's order.

Sometimes the terms avoidable and unavoidable costs are used instead of relevant and irrelevant cost. An avoidable cost is one which is saved by not choosing a decision, so it is equivalent to a relevant cost. In the brilliant example above, the £100 material cost is unavoidable (as it has been incurred already) and is thus irrelevant. A further term you might encounter is sunk cost.

**brilliant** definition

A **sunk cost** is a cost which has been made as a result of a prior decision and is unaffected by future decisions.

Sunk costs are irrelevant for decision-making. For example, if a business buys a new piece of equipment for £50,000, this cost is sunk regardless of scrap value or estimated life of the equipment. Similarly, the £100 material cost in the earlier brilliant example is also a sunk cost.

Finally, many business decisions involve consideration of lost opportunities if one course of action is selected over another.

**brilliant** definition

An **opportunity cost** is one which measures the loss or sacrifice of one course of action over another.

If you have ever studied economics, you'll know just how much this discipline loves to talk about opportunity costs. To give a simple example, the opportunity costs of working are things like spending less time with your family. Businesses also need to consider opportunity costs, as depicted in the following example.

**brilliant** example

A business gets an opportunity to supply a customer they have been trying to do business with. The profit from the order is £1,000. To supply the customer, another order will need to be cancelled, losing £200 profit. Thus the opportunity cost of taking the order will be £200, and the net profit £800.

Of course, in the above example, the opportunity cost may be one worth suffering for the likelihood of future business. For the decision in the example though, the opportunity cost needs to be considered to give the best possible information on which to make the decision.

You now know how costs can be classified and used in making day-to-day business decisions. One of the most important decisions for any business is the price of its product or service. Any of the cost classifications you now know may be relevant to calculating a product or service cost, but more importantly you need to be sure that you set a price high enough to cover all costs. Let's now explore briefly some issues when product costs need to be worked out.

## Costing a product or service

Let's assume a business makes a product with two direct costs, namely materials and labour. The business also has overhead costs. You might think it's quite easy then to calculate the cost of making the product by simply capturing the cost of all materials used, the time worked (to calculate labour cost) and add in the overhead cost. Well, it's not all that easy and you need to understand a little more, which I'll outline below. What is described below is what management accountants refer to as job costing.

 **brilliant** definition

Job costing is a technique used to capture the full cost of a unit of output where units of output differ.

A computer manufacturer like Dell or HP is a good example of a business using job costing. Each PC or Notebook sold is normally configured to customer order requirements, so the outputs differ each time.

## Material costs

When a product is made and materials are used in the process, the material cost can be attributed to the full cost. But what if the price of the materials varies? For example, a business may have a number of suppliers. Even if there is only one supplier, then prices can go up or down. Or to complicate matters even further, what happens if prices of materials fluctuate because they are bought in a foreign currency? These kinds of issues may mean that at any one time, a business may have a stock of the same materials which have been purchased at different costs. The question then is, what cost is used in the product cost?

The answer to this question is that accountants make assumptions about how materials are used. From these assumptions, cost of materials used in a product/service can be determined. The assumptions are detailed below:

- **First-In-First-Out (FIFO)** Under FIFO, it is assumed that the oldest materials are used first. Therefore, the material cost will be at the oldest price paid.
- **Last-In-First-Out (LIFO)** Under LIFO, it is assumed that the newest materials are used first. This means that the material cost will be at the most recent price.
- **Average cost (AVCO)** Under this method, a weighted average cost is calculated of all material costs. This means that the material cost will be reflective of the mixed prices paid for materials.

No matter which assumption is used, I should point out that these assumptions are used by accountants to establish a material cost. These methods do not relate to the physical movement of goods, although in terms of managing old stock of any kind a FIFO approach would be a good idea.

As management accounting is not regulated in any way, internally a business could choose any of the above methods to obtain the material cost element of product cost. However, taxation and financial accounting rules do not permit the use of the LIFO method. Any ideas why? Jot your answer down on a piece of paper before reading on.

The answer relates to how the material cost used affects profit. Remember from Chapter 4 that gross profit is sales less cost of sales. And, one component of cost of sales is the closing stock figure. Remember that the closing stock value is deducted, so the lower the stock value, the higher the cost of sales. In turn, a higher cost of sales means a lower profit. If material were valued using a LIFO method, then profits would be lower as the stocks of materials are assumed to be at the oldest price.

In practice the AVCO method is a quite common way to calculate the material cost component of product cost. Many accounting software packages can do the work of costing materials for a business, but this functionality usually means the more expensive version of software is required. If a business has high volumes of materials and other components in stock, such a system is essential.

## Labour costs

By and large, labour costs do not pose many problems in job costing, other than ensuring that time worked is accurately recorded. Time worked on a job can be recorded manually on a 'job card' or more commonly nowadays, entered into a computerised production/job control system. The only other complication is to cost labour at the correct hourly rate, which might include additional pay for overtime for example.

## Overhead costs

Overhead costs are, as mentioned earlier, all other indirect costs involved in making a product or service. Although an indirect cost cannot be easily attributed to a product or service, some effort must be made to do so. Otherwise, the full product cost would not be apparent and it would be difficult to work out what price to sell at. In fact, calculating a portion of overhead cost for a product or service is one of the problem issues in management accounting. I'll now describe what is referred to as the 'traditional method' of allocating overhead costs. In fact, what you know at this point about calculating product cost (i.e. material, labour and overhead) is referred to as absorption costing.

 **brilliant** definition

**Absorption costing** is a method of calculating the cost of manufacturing a product or providing a service. The cost calculated includes material, labour and all manufacturing overhead.

You'll notice from the definition above that only manufacturing overhead is included. This is okay for the moment and I'll return to this point below. For now, the question is how do we make an effort to include manufacturing overhead costs in the cost of a product/service? Using absorption costing, the basic idea is to use a planned or budgeted overhead figure (see Chapter 9 for more on budgeting) and spread this cost across all planned units of output. Here's an example to help you understand.

 **brilliant** example

Suppose a business expects its manufacturing overhead to be £100,000 of the next year. It also plans to make 25,000 of its product. This means that the manufacturing overhead cost for each product will be £4 (£100,000/25,000).

The calculated overhead rate, £4 in the above example, is applied to (or absorbed by) each product. You might ask, but what if output is not 25,000 and actual overheads are more or less than planned? This of course happens all the time as nobody can plan with certainty for the future. Here's another example which explains what happens.

**brilliant** example

Suppose the business in the previous example actually made 26,000 products and actual overhead was £108,000. Remember the absorption rate was £4 per product. As 26,000 products were made, a total of £104,000 (26,000 × £4) of manufacturing overhead has been included in products costs. This means there is a shortfall of £4,000 (£108,000 − £104,000) compared to actual cost. This £4,000 of 'under-absorbed' overhead is not reabsorbed into the product cost, but is shown in the income statement as an expense.

As you'll notice from the above example, absorption costing is not perfect. It also traditionally only includes manufacturing overhead. Other overhead costs like selling and administrative overheads were not traditionally absorbed – instead they were simply put in the income statement. This is because selling and administrative overheads were traditionally less relevant. However, in modern businesses this may not be so and it is possible to include all overheads when calculating an absorption rate. However, if total overhead cost is allocated based on budgeted output (as in the above examples) or on labour hours worked (another possible way), this might have no relationship at all with how overheads like selling and administrative overheads actually arise. Another problem with absorption costing is that it assumes output is similar. Nowadays, product diversity is more normal in businesses. An alternative method of allocating overhead called activity-based costing is often used. I won't explain activity-based costing here, but what it does is it collects overhead cost by business activity (e.g. sales, design, logistics) and allocates overhead cost to products/services based on how much of each activity it uses. For example, a product which requires a new design would get a portion of the design activities overhead cost. Other products not requiring a new design would have no design cost attributed. Thus, activity-based costing may address the two mentioned flaws of traditional absorption costing.

For a basic understanding of costs, the method used to allocate overhead cost to products/services does not matter so much. What is important is that some effort is made to include as many direct and indirect costs as possible in the calculation of the product or service cost. This is particularly important when trying to determine a price. You already know that fixed costs, such as overheads, are not relevant to all business decisions, but are to setting a price. In the next chapter, you'll learn a little more about the interactions of costs, prices and output.

 **brilliant** recap

- A cost is a monetary measure of resources sacrificed or forgone.
- Costs can be classified in a number of ways – by how they behave when output changes, by their relevance to products or services, or by relevance to decisions.
- When costing a product or service, material, labour and overhead costs should be included.
- Absorption costing is a traditional technique often used to apportion manufacturing overhead to products/services.

**CHAPTER 9**

# Budgeting basics

The only relevant test of the validity of a hypothesis is comparison of prediction with experience.

*Milton Friedman, economist*

The above brilliant words from American economist Milton Friedman suggest that a plan should be monitored to see what actually happens. Businesses plan regularly, so now that you know about costs from Chapter 8, in this chapter you'll learn how to plan for future costs and revenues. First, you'll learn what a budget is and how to prepare various budgets for a business. I'll then give you a brief summary of how the plans are used as a possible control mechanism in an organisation. Finally, I introduce another useful planning and decision-making technique called cost-volume-profit (CVP) analysis, which is a really simple and useful tool for any business manager or accountant.

## What is a budget?

A budget is simply a plan for the future expressed in money terms. I'm sure you're aware of the annual budget a government makes, or that you have to 'budget' your own outgoings to make sure you don't run short at the end of the week or month. In the same way, a business needs to plan for the future so that it can avoid running short of money and other resources. As a minimum, I recommend any business has at least a budget for its revenue and major costs. It is always better to have more detail, but in smaller businesses this might not make sense given the time available to the owners. Let's see how to prepare some of the main budgets.

## Preparing budgets

As I mentioned above, a budget is a plan. This means that we can never be certain that what we plan actually happens, and the next section deals with this. However, even a bad plan is better than no plan at all. Like any plan, certain assumptions have to be made of course when preparing a budget and once any assumptions are reasonable, you're off to a good start.

## Budgeting for sales

The first budget any business normally prepares is the sales budget. You might be thinking, should I not plan for costs first and then work out my planned selling price? The answer is yes, you do need to do this separately, and I'll deal with this later. The reason for starting with a sales budget is to ensure a business can either make or buy what it plans to sell, and from this work out the costs. So, there is a bit of capacity planning going on in the background. This makes a lot of sense as any problems, such as not having enough money to buy the stock you hope to sell, or not having enough storage space, are identified early.

Preparing a sales budget is probably one of the easier tasks in creating a budget. All you need do is have a selling price you hope to sell products at and the quantity you hope to sell. Let's have a look at an example. Figure 9.1 shows a sales budget for a fictitious business, John's Manufacturing.

| John's Manufacturing | | | |
|---|---|---|---|
| Sales budget | | | |
| | January | February | March |
| Units | 1,200 | 1,300 | 1,150 |
| Price £ | 20.00 | 21.00 | 19.00 |
| Sales budget £ | 24,000 | 27,300 | 21,850 |

Figure 9.1 Sales budget for John's Manufacturing

As you can see in this example, I have shown a sales budget for three months only – to fit it on a page and keep things readable. Normally, a budget would be prepared for a year. The sales budget is, as you can see, a simple matter of estimating the sales price and the units to be sold. The budget sales units can be determined by estimating volumes to be sold to customers, which means undertaking a detailed analysis of what can be sold to each customer. Sales representatives or other sales staff might be quite helpful during this task.

# Budgeting for product costs

Once a sales budget is prepared, the next stage is to work out budgets for costs. We'll now build on the John's Manufacturing example. As the name of the business suggests, we'll assume that the business manufactures rather than buys its products. The next step then is to work out budgets for the cost of production. First, here is some additional information (which you'll need to refer back to).

### Additional information for John's Manufacturing

| | |
|---|---|
| Finished units in stock, 1 January | 400 |
| Materials (kg) in stock, 1 January | 600 |
| Materials (kg) used per unit produced | 2.5 |
| Material cost per kg | £3.00 |
| Labour cost per unit | £1.50 |
| Manufacturing overhead cost per unit | £1.20 |
| Sales and administration overhead (per month) | £5,000 |
| A stock of finished goods of 30% of sales is to be maintained | |
| A stock of materials of 20% of production is to be maintained | |

## Budgeting for production quantities

As the information given above shows, there are some goods already held at the beginning of January, 400 units. Additionally, a stock of finished goods of 30% of sales is to be maintained. Take a look at Figure 9.2.

You can see in January for example, that the first figure (1,200 units) comes from the sales budget in Figure 9.1. Since 400 units are already in stock, this is deducted and then 30% of the sales figure (1,200 × 30% = 360 units)

| John's Manufacturing | | | |
|---|---|---|---|
| *Production budget* | | | |
| | January | February | March |
| Required for sales (see Figure 9.1) | 1,200 | 1,300 | 1,150 |
| Beginning stock | (400) | (360) | (390) |
| Required ending stock (30%) | 360 | 390 | 345 |
| Production quantity | 1,160 | 1,330 | 1,105 |

Figure 9.2  Production budget for John's Manufacturing

is added to arrive at the figure that needs to be produced. So, in January, 1,160 units must be manufactured. This process repeats for each month.

## Budgeting for materials, labour and overhead cost

Now that the quantity to be produced is known (Figure 9.2), the next step is to prepare budgets for the costs of production. Using the information above, we'll now prepare a budget for material, labour and overhead costs.

First, to prepare a material cost budget we can use the units produced figure as a starting point. As with finished goods, John's Manufacturing also has some stocks of materials, so we need to take this into account as above in the production budget. Figure 9.3 shows the materials to be used in production and the budgeted costs.

| John's Manufacturing | | | |
|---|---|---|---|
| *Materials usage and purchase budget* | | | |
| | January | February | March |
| Production units (see Figure 9.2) | 1,160 | 1,330 | 1,105 |
| Kg material per unit | 2.5 | 2.5 | 2.5 |
| Kg material material | 2,900 | 3,325 | 2,763 |
| Beginning stock kg | (600) | (232) | (266) |
| Ending stock kg (20% production) | 232 | 266 | 221 |
| Purchase requirements | 2,532 | 3,359 | 2,718 |
| Price per kg (£) | 3 | 3 | 3 |
| Budget material costs | 7,596 | 10,077 | 8,153 |

Figure 9.3  Material usage and cost budget for John's Manufacturing

The starting point is units produced. Looking at the month of January as an example, we start with the units to be produced: 1,160 units. Earlier,

we were told that each unit needs 2.5kg of material, so 2,900kg (1,160 ×
2.5) are needed to meet the production requirements for January. Again,
there are some materials in stock (600kg) which are deducted and a
policy of keeping material stocks at 20% of production. This means that
2,532kg of materials are required. Once the materials required for use in
production are known, then a simple multiplication by the price gives a
material cost budget.

Budgeting for labour cost is relatively simple, once the time taken to make
each unit is known. Briefly, the labour time per unit might be worked out
by meticulously recording how long it takes an employee to do the work.
With the labour time known, the pay rate of employees can be incorpo-
rated to work out a labour budget, as shown in Figure 9.4.

**John's Manufacturing**

*Labour cost budget*

| | January | February | March |
|---|---|---|---|
| Production units (see Figure 9.2) | 1,160 | 1,330 | 1,105 |
| Labour cost per unit | 1.50 | 1.50 | 1.50 |
| Labour cost | 1,740 | 1,995 | 1,658 |
| | | | |
| *Overhead cost budget* | | | |
| Production units (see Figure 9.2) | 1,160 | 1,330 | 1,105 |
| Labour cost per unit | 1.20 | 1.20 | 1.20 |
| Labour cost | 1,392 | 1,596 | 1,326 |

Figure 9.4  Labour and overhead cost budget for John's Manufacturing

Of course, in practice preparing a labour budget might be a time-
consuming task given many different tasks and pay rates in a business.

Budgeting for overhead is simple enough too once we have already calculated an overhead rate (see the brilliant example on p. 150). In the case
of John's Manufacturing, we are given an overhead cost per unit, so we
simply multiply this cost by the units to be produced – see Figure 9.4
above.

At this point, we can now prepare a budgeted profit statement. Before
doing this, let's think for a moment about preparing a budget for a business that simply purchases goods rather than manufactures them. In
this case, the budgeting process is a little simpler. In essence, the budget
would be similar to the materials usage and cost budget shown in Figure

9.3. Materials in stock would be included as in Figure 9.3, and also any minimum stock holding requirements. No labour or overhead budgets as in Figure 9.4 are required.

# A budgeted profit statement

Now let's bring all the budgets and information on John's Manufacturing together to prepare a budgeted profit statement, as shown in Figure 9.5.

**John's Manufacturing**

*Budgeted profit statement*

| | January | February | March | Total |
|---|---|---|---|---|
| Sales | 24,000 | 27,300 | 21,850 | 73,150 |
| *Cost of sales* | | | | |
| Opening stock of finshed goods (see note) | 2,280 | 2,052 | 2,223 | 2,280 |
| Material costs | 7,596 | 10,077 | 8,153 | 25,826 |
| Labour costs | 1,740 | 1,995 | 1,658 | 5,393 |
| Overhead | 1,392 | 1,596 | 1,326 | 4,314 |
| Closing stock of finished goods (see note) | (2,052) | (2,223) | (1,968) | (1,968) |
| | 10,956 | 13,497 | 11,392 | 35,845 |
| Sales and administration overhead | 5,000 | 5,000 | 5,000 | 15,000 |
| Total Costs | 15,956 | 18,497 | 16,392 | 50,845 |
| Budgeted profit/(loss) | 8,044 | 8,803 | 5,458 | 22,305 |
| **Note:** | | | | |
| Stock at start of month (see Figure 9.2) | 400 | 360 | 390 | |
| Cost per unit | 5.70 | 5.70 | 5.70 | |
| Opening stock value | 2,280 | 2,052 | 2,223 | |
| Stock at end of month (see Figure 9.2) | 360 | 390 | 345 | |
| Cost per unit | 5.70 | 5.70 | 5.70 | |
| Closing stock value | 2,052 | 2,223 | 1,968 | |

Figure 9.5 Budgeted profit statement for John's Manufacturing

As you can see in Figure 9.5, a budgeted profit statement is simply the bringing together of all costs and income. You'll see I've included a note below to show how the value of opening and closing stocks is calculated. The cost per unit of £5.70 (material, labour and overhead) is used to value stock – remember in Chapter 4 (see p. 75), you learned that stocks (inventory) are valued at the lower of cost or net realisable value. I have also added in the monthly sales and administration overhead costs. The end result is a budgeted profit figure for each month and the quarter. In practice a business might also have a sum for the year. Note also that in the total column, the values for opening and closing stocks of finished goods refer to the first and last month respectively (i.e. January and March).

# Budgeting for cash flow

You already know that accounting is based in the accruals concept, not on when cash is paid. But, cash is very important to any business. You'll learn in Chapter 10 that the survival of any business is dependent on its ability to have sufficient cash to pay debts as they fall due. With this in mind, most businesses will prepare a cash budget too. With the budgets for sales and costs done, with a few more assumptions we can prepare a cash budget for John's Manufacturing. Here's some more information we'll need.

## Additional data on John's Manufacturing

Sales are 40% cash, 60% on credit

Credit customers pay one month after sale

Customers owe £5,500 at the end of December

Suppliers of materials are paid two months after purchase, labour and overheads are paid in month incurred

Suppliers are owed £800 from November and £1,000 from December

Equipment costing £30,000 will be bought and paid for in March

The balance of cash in the bank on 1 January was £2,500

Now let's see how we can use the budgets already prepared and this additional information to prepare a cash budget. Remember, the key thing a cash budget does is plan for cash inflows and outflows. If something is not cash, it does not appear in the cash budget – depreciation or accruals, for example. Figure 9.6 shows the cash budget for John's Manufacturing.

You can see how each month the cash inflows and outflows are shown, and the difference between them is a net cash flow in or out of the business. The net cash flow is added to the cash balance at the beginning of the month to work out the closing cash balance. You'll see the purchase of the equipment in March is shown in full – this would not be so under the

| *John's Manufacturing* | | | | |
|---|---|---|---|---|
| *Cash budget* | | | | |
| *Cash receipts* | January | February | March | Total |
| Sales | | | | |
| Cash sales 40% | 9,600 | 10,920 | 8,740 | 29,260 |
| Credit sales 60%, 1 month after sale | 5,500 | 14,400 | 16,380 | 36,280 |
| | 15,100 | 25,320 | 25,120 | 65,540 |
| *Cash payments* | | | | |
| Materials, 2 months after purchase | (800) | (1,000) | (7,596) | (9,396) |
| Labour | (1,740) | (1,995) | (1,658) | (5,393) |
| Overheads (incl. selling & admin.) | (6,392) | (6,596) | (6,326) | (19,314) |
| Purchase of equipment | | | (30,000) | (30,000) |
| | (8,932) | (9,591) | (45,580) | (64,103) |
| Net cash flow | 6,168 | 15,729 | (20,460) | 1,438 |
| Opening balance | 2,500 | 8,668 | 24,397 | 2,500 |
| Closing balance | 8,668 | 24,397 | 3,938 | 3,938 |

Figure 9.6 Cash budget for John's Manufacturing

accruals concept in accounting. In this example, the cash balances remain positive, which is of course good. However, when a business prepares a cash budget, it might find that some months might show a negative cash balance. If this is so, then at least remedies can be sought in advance, for example you can collect money faster from customers or seek a bank overdraft. Cash budgets are quite important for any business and may be prepared on a more frequent basis than other budgets.

## Pros and cons of budgets

Preparing budgets for a business has a number of advantages:

1 Budgets force a business to plan, or think about the future. Planning is an essential component of running any business.

2 Preparing budgets means parts of a business must communicate and co-ordinate well. For example, sales staff might work closely with purchasing or production staff to ensure what they plan to sell can be manufactured or bought.

3 Once created, budgets are a control and evaluation tool for comparison with actual results (see more below).

There are also some disadvantages. One of the main issues is that all budgets are based on key assumptions. With some good research, as business owner/manager you should be able to make a best guess of things like projected selling price, but it is only a guess. A further problem with budgeting is that budgets can place too much emphasis on short-term costs. For example, if costs are to be cut to keep within budget, a business might cut back on things like training. This might be a problem in the longer term.

No matter the size of business, plans or budgets will be prepared. Even a small first-time business will have to prepare a budget as part of a business plan if it is seeking finance from a bank or government agency. Larger businesses will have quite formal budgeting procedures in place, but the principles are the same no matter the size of business.

## Budgets as a control tool

As mentioned above, one of the advantages of preparing budgets is that they can be used as a control tool. Once a budget has been prepared, it can be reviewed regularly to assess the plan versus what actually happens. For example, the budgets prepared for John's Manufacturing in this chapter have been prepared by month. Therefore, at the end of each month, the budget and actual information can be compared. Then, reasons for the differences can be sought out and perhaps budgets for the following months changed to reflect what needs to be achieved to make up sales shortfalls or cost over-runs for example. Let's see how budgets can be used as a control and performance evaluation tool.

To use budgets as a control tool they have to be reviewed regularly. This means two things – compare the budget to actual results and review whether or not the budget was right. However, before doing any comparison of budget to actual figures, a little bit of work is needed. Have a look back at Figure 9.4 and the labour cost budget for John's Manufacturing. Now suppose actual labour costs for January were £ 1,860 and actual units produced were 1,200. If we compare just the costs for now, the actual labour cost is £120 more than the budget (£1,860 − £1,740). But is this a fair comparison? Jot down what you think overleaf:

---

---

The answer is no. The reason for this is that we are not comparing like with like. The original budget predicted an output of 1,160 units, whereas the actual output was 1,200 units. The solution is to re-draft or 'flex' the budget to reflect the actual quantity. In effect this is setting the budget to what it would have been had we known the actual output level. Figure 9.7 shows the labour budget, which has been flexed to the actual output level of 1,200 units.

| *John's Manufacturing* | | | |
|---|---|---|---|
| *Labour costs – January* | Original budget | Flexed budget | Actual |
| Production units | 1,160 | 1,200 | 1,200 |
| Labour costs per unit | 1.50 | 1.50 | |
| Labour cost | 1,740 | 1,800 | 1,860 |

Figure 9.7  A flexed labour budget for John's Manufacturing

Looking at Figure 9.7, it would be better to compare the actual labour cost of £1,860 with the flexed budget value of £1,800, thus showing that labour costs were still over budget but by less. The next step, in practice, would be to find out why labour costs are higher. This is beyond the scope of this book, but it could be factors like a higher pay rate or poor productivity. The original budget for all costs and revenues should be flexed each time a comparison is required. Then you can spot areas where a large difference exists and start to examine the causes. This process is called variance analysis and is again beyond the scope of this book, but briefly differences can occur for two main reasons: 1) the budgets were poorly formulated, or 2) an element of the business operations is potentially not well-managed.

The very act of comparing actual with budget is also a means of measuring performance. As already mentioned above, any difference shown between a flexed budget and actual results may indicate that performance is not as good (or better) than planned. A business could also compare its performance against budget year on year. It might also be possible to compare budgets and actual results with competitors or industry benchmarks. Businesses often pay staff based on performance against a budget or plan, so this is yet another reason for comparing actual and budget figures and ensuring that the budget itself is as accurate as possible – which means it may need regular updating.

Regardless of size, a business is unlikely to survive without some form of budget or plan. Budgets may be more or less complicated than what you've learned here, but the key point is to plan in some way for the future.

## Cost-volume-profit analysis

Now that you know about cost classifications and budgets, there is a very useful technique called cost-volume-profit (CVP) analysis which is useful to know. This technique is often used to help business planning, as well as to check the effects of changes in cost or output on overall profits. Take a look at Figure 9.8, which shows how to calculate profit for a business.

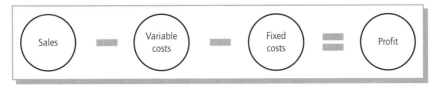

Figure 9.8  Calculating profit in a business

Now, a question for you. What will profit be when a business breaks even? Nil is the correct answer, as break-even means a business makes neither a profit nor loss. If profit is nil, then we say the business breaks even. Or, put another way, sales less variable costs will equal fixed costs, as shown in Figure 9.9.

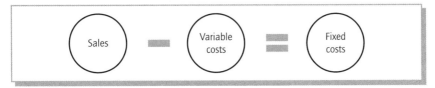

Figure 9.9  Costs and revenues when a business breaks even

 **brilliant** definition

Break-even is the output level at which a business makes neither a profit nor a loss.

Now, for another question. When a business prepares a budget, wouldn't it be useful to know how many units of the product/service need to be sold to break even? This would be a really useful minimum target for any business. Or in the start-up phase of a business, knowing a break-even sales point might be very useful for a business plan. Break-even can be worked out quite easily, but first you need to know about a management accounting term, contribution.

 **brilliant** definition

Contribution is selling price less all variable costs.

Contribution can be calculated for a product/service or in total. Take a look back at Figure 9.9 and you'll notice the left-hand side of the figure is equal to contribution. Logically, the greater the contribution, the more fixed costs are covered by sales and profits are made. We could represent the left-hand side of Figure 9.9 as follows:

Contribution per unit × number of units sold

Taking the above, we can derive Figure 9.10.

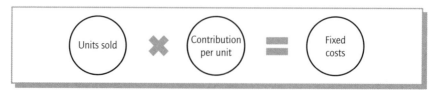

Figure 9.10 Contribution per unit versus fixed costs

You know that for a business to break even, the units sold times the contribution per unit must equal fixed costs, i.e. the left and right of Figure 9.10 must be the same. Thus, if we want to calculate the units we need to sell to break even, we can rearrange Figure 9.10 as shown in Figure 9.11.

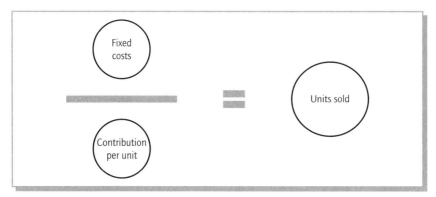

Figure 9.11  A formula for break-even

From this formula, if fixed costs and the contribution per unit of product/ service are known, it is possible to quickly work out how many units of the product/service need to be sold to break even. This formula can also be used to quickly assess the impact of any change in cost or price on the break-even sales volume too. Have a look at the following brilliant example.

 **example**

A business sells its product for £100 and has variable costs of £40 per unit. It has fixed costs of £600,000. The break-even sales units for the business are thus:

$$\frac{£600,000}{£60} = 10,000 \text{ units}$$

Now let's assume the business wants to increase sale volume through a promotional campaign. It is not possible to increase the selling price and the promotional campaign will cost £50,000.

The additional cost of the promotion is a fixed cost, so let's recalculate the break-even sales level.

$$\frac{£600,000 + £50,000}{£60} = 10,833 \text{ units}$$

The business must therefore sell an additional 833 units to cover the cost of the promotion. The question for the business now is, 'Is this increase in sales possible?' If not, then the promotional campaign might not be worthwhile.

The above example shows just one possible use of the break-even formula. Any changes in sales price, variable or fixed costs can be plugged into the formula to see the effect on sales volume. I think you'll appreciate how knowledge of this break-even technique is of great benefit to any business. It allows the effects of business decisions to be quickly assessed, and thus, decisions can be made quite quickly.

## brilliant recap

- A budget is a plan for the future, normally expressed in money terms.
- Budgets should be prepared for revenues and costs.
- Preparing a cash budget is important as it may identify times when cash flow is poor in advance.
- Budgets force businesses to plan for the future.
- On the downside, a budget is as good as its key assumptions.
- Once prepared, budgets can be used to help control and measure the performance of a business.
- Cost-volume-profit (break-even) techniques are very useful for decision-making. The technique(s) allow a manager/business owner/accountant to quickly assess any changes in cost or price on break-even sales volume.

# PART 4

# Interpreting and using financial statements – what outsiders do

# CHAPTER 10

# Analysing financial statements

ou now know how financial statements are prepared, so the next step is to appreciate what they are telling you about a business. For example, you might want an answer to the following questions:

- Can I earn a better return on my money by investing it elsewhere?
- How is my business performing compared to other similar businesses?

You might also want to assess the financial state of a business you want to buy, which I'll detail more in Chapter 11. In accounting, it is possible to give answers to such questions by comparing and analysing financial statements. In essence, what we are trying to do is to make the numbers in the financial statements 'tell the story' of how a business is performing over time.

## Comparing financial statements

You learned in Chapter 6, that company financial statements show two years' figures (i.e. comparatives) in the income statement and balance sheet. This is a requirement of accounting regulations and company law. You might think that comparing this year's results with last year's (or results for earlier years) can provide a useful trend over time, and it does. But there are some difficulties with this. The most obvious problem is that the figures are historic. Figures such as sales revenue might show a trend upwards, but prices generally rise due to inflation anyway. So how relevant is it to say that revenues rose by 3% when inflation is also 3%? In this example, revenues in real terms did not grow at all. Another difficulty is that one figure on its own or a trend in a figure may give a false impression. Have a look at the following figures:

|  | £m |
|---|---|
| Company A profit | 50 |
| Company B profit | 100 |

Before reading on, jot down here which company you think is more profitable. __

Considering only the numbers, company B is the answer as it has a more profit. This is misleading as the money (capital) invested to achieve the profit needs to be considered too. Here's some additional information on the assets of each business.

|  | Profit £m | Assets £m |
|---|---|---|
| Company A | 50 | 200 |
| Company B | 100 | 500 |

Now, by expressing the profit as a percentage of assets, it is easy to see the picture has changed. Company A makes a return on the invested capital of 25% (£50m/£200), whereas Company B makes a return of 20% (£100m/£500m). Thus, Company A, despite having half the profit levels in £s of Company B, is actually making better use of its capital.

A final difficulty in comparing financial statements is that not all businesses are the same. To compare the financial statements of an airline like Ryanair with those of an automotive company like Honda does not make a lot of sense as the underlying businesses are completely different. Even within the same industry comparisons can be tenuous. Both Ryanair and British Airways are airlines, but each company operates a very different business model. Ryanair tends to operate on a low cost, no frills basis, whereas British Airways offers a more traditional service based on quality and flexibility.

With knowledge of the limitations in comparing financial statements, let's now see how financial statements can be used to paint a picture of a business. In Chapter 1, you learned the many users of accounting information; business owners, lenders, customers, suppliers, tax authorities and potential investors. All these users may have differing reasons for using financial statements. To make some sense of financial statements, accountants, business owners, investors and other users frequently use what is called financial ratio analysis. By using ratios, it is possible to eliminate the problem of the scale of numbers (i.e. £1 as a percentage of £10 is 10% in the same way that £1m as a percentage of £10m is 10%). You'll now learn these ratios and see that some are more important to certain users of financial statements.

## Financial ratios

Financial ratios can be calculated in three broad areas;

1 profitability
2 efficiency and liquidity
3 gearing and investment.

To help you appreciate these financial ratios, we'll use the income state-ment and balance sheet of a fictional company called Systera plc (shown in Figure 10.1) to calculate and interpret ratios.

In total, you'll learn how to calculate 15 ratios, all of which are shown in Figure 10.2. I'll explain each ratio in turn, but you might need to flick back to both Figures 10.1 and 10.2 as the chapter progresses. The ratios calculated are based on two years of financial statements. In practice, you might want to look at longer-term trends to get a full picture and remove the possibility of any one-off blips.

## Analysing profitability

The objective of profitability ratios is to give an indication of the return (profit) on the investment in a business. Before looking at some ratios, think about what is the minimum return on investment a business would deem acceptable? The answer to this question is not an easy one. Each business (and its owners) may have their own outlook on a required return. Expected returns are related to risk too so, for example, bank deposit accounts give a low rate of return – the interest rate is normally quite low, but there is typically little or no risk attached. However, a stock market investment may gain a higher level of return, but the risk is much greater – anyone who invested in bank shares in recent years can testify to this.

A reasonable answer to what is a good return might be something greater than the rate available from putting money on deposit and closer to the

Income statement of Systera Corporation plc

|  | 31/12/2010 | | 31/12/2009 | |
|---|---|---|---|---|
| Sales |  | 501,200 |  | 435,800 |
| *Cost of sales* |  |  |  |  |
| Opening stock | 50,300 |  | 47,000 |  |
| Purchases | 199,900 |  | 192,200 |  |
| Closing stock | (47,300) |  | (42,600) |  |
|  |  | 202,900 |  | 196,600 |
| *Gross profit* |  | 298,300 |  | 239,200 |
| Distribution costs | 40,000 |  | 36,700 |  |
| Administration expenses | 55,700 |  | 49,700 |  |
| Finance costs | 11,800 |  | 11,300 |  |
|  |  | 107,500 |  | 97,700 |
| Net profit/(loss) |  | 190,800 |  | 141,500 |
| Taxation |  | (26,700) |  | (14,200) |
| *Profit after tax* |  | 164,100 |  | 127,300 |
| Dividends |  | (16,200) |  | (11,200) |
| Retained profits |  | 147,900 |  | 116,100 |
| Profits brought forward |  | 503,800 |  | 387,700 |
| Profits carried forward |  | 651,700 |  | 503,800 |

(Note: all sales and purchases are on credit. Finance costs consist of loan interest.)

Balance sheet of Systera Corporation plc

|  | 31/12/2010 | | 31/12/2009 | |
|---|---|---|---|---|
| Non-current assets |  | 861,000 |  | 626,400 |
| **Current assets** |  |  |  |  |
| Inventories | 47,300 |  | 42,600 |  |
| Trade receivables | 63,100 |  | 59,900 |  |
| Bank | 48,600 |  | 61,200 |  |
|  | 159,000 |  | 163,700 |  |
| **Current liabilities** |  |  |  |  |
| Trade payables | 63,600 |  | 51,100 |  |
| Other accruals | 11,400 |  | 14,600 |  |
|  | 75,000 |  | 65,700 |  |
| Net current assets/(liabilities) |  | 84,000 |  | 98,000 |
|  |  | 945,000 |  | 724,400 |
| **Equity** |  |  |  |  |
| Ordinary £1 shares |  | 191,900 |  | 119,200 |
| Retained profits |  | 651,700 |  | 503,800 |
|  |  | 843,600 |  | 623,000 |
| **Non-current liabilities** |  |  |  |  |
| Loans |  | 101,400 |  | 101,400 |
|  |  | 945,000 |  | 724,400 |

The market value of shares in Systera plc was £8.75 at the end of 2010, and £6.45 at the end of 2009.

Figure 10.1 Income statement and balance sheet of Systera plc

| Profitability ratios | 31/12/2010 | | 31/12/2009 | |
|---|---|---|---|---|
| *Return on Capital employed (ROCE) (%)* | | | | |
| Profit (before interest and tax) x 100 / Capital employed | 202,600 x 100 = 945,000 | 21.44% | 152,800 x 100 = 724,400 | 21.09% |
| *Profit margin (%)* | | | | |
| Profit (before interest and tax) x 100 / Sales | 202,600 x 100 = 501,200 | 40.42% | 152,800 x 100 = 435,800 | 35.06% |
| *Asset turnover (times)* | | | | |
| Sales / Total assets (capital employed) | 501,200 / 945,000 = | 0.530 | 435,800 x 100 = 724,400 | 0.602 |
| *Gross profit margin (%)* | | | | |
| Gross profit x 100 / Sales | 298,300 x 100 = 501,200 | 59.52% | 239,200 x 100 = 435,800 | 54.89% |
| *Total expenses to sales (%)* | | | | |
| Total expenses x 100 / Sales | 107,500 x 100 = 501,200 | 21.45% | 97,700 x 100 = 435,800 | 22.42% |
| *Return on shareholder funds (%)* | | | | |
| Profit after tax and preference dividends x 100 / Ordinary share capital + reserves | 164,100 x 100 = 843,600 | 19.45% | 127,300 x 100 = 623,000 | 20.43% |
| **Working capital ratios** | | | | |
| *Inventory turnover (times)* | | | | |
| Cost of sales / Average stock | 202,900 / 48,800 = | 4.158 | 196,600 / 44,800 = | 4.388 |
| * Average stock is the average of opening and closing stocks | | | | |
| *Average credit period allowed (days)* | | | | |
| Trade receivables x 365 / Credit sales | 63,100 x 365 = 501,200 | 46.0 | 59,900 x 365 435,800 | 50.2% |
| *Average credit period received (days)* | | | | |
| Trade payables x 365 / Credit purchases | 63,600 x 365 = 199,900 | 116.1 | 51,200 x 365 = 192,200 | 97.0 |
| **Liquidity ratios** | | | | |
| *Current ratio* | | | | |
| Current assets / Current liabilities | 159,000 / 75,000 = | 2.12:1 | 163,700 / 65,700 = | 2.49:1 |

| *Liquid (acid test/quick) ratio* | | | | | |
| --- | --- | --- | --- | --- | --- |
| Current assets − inventories / Current liabilities | $\frac{111{,}700}{75{,}000}$ = | 1.49:1 | $\frac{121{,}100}{65{,}700}$ = | 1.84:1 |
| **Investment ratios** | | | | | |
| *Debt/equity ratio* | | | | | |
| Debt / Equity | $\frac{101{,}400}{843{,}600}$ = | 0.12:1 | $\frac{101{,}400}{623{,}000}$ = | 0.16:1 |
| *Interest cover (times)* | | | | | |
| Profit before interest / Interest | $\frac{202{,}600}{11{,}800}$ = | 17.17 | $\frac{152{,}800}{11{,}300}$ = | 13.52 |
| *Earning per share (£)* | | | | | |
| Profit after tax and preference dividend / No. of ordinary shares in issue | $\frac{164{,}100}{191{,}900}$ = | 0.86 | $\frac{127{,}300}{119{,}200}$ = | 1.07 |
| *Price earnings (times)* | | | | | |
| Market price per share / Earning per share | $\frac{8.75}{0.86}$ = | 10.23 | $\frac{6.45}{1.07}$ = | 6.04 |
| *Dividend cover (times)* | | | | | |
| Profit after tax and preference dividend / Total ordinary dividend | $\frac{164{,}100}{16{,}200}$ = | 10.13 | $\frac{127{,}300}{11{,}200}$ = | 11.37 |

Figure 10.2  Ratio analysis of Systera plc

return from riskier activity like investing in the stock market. With this in mind, to compare the profitability of a business to anything, we could consider the risk-free deposit rate as an absolute minimum expected return.

Now let's see how to calculate some profitability ratios. The first ratio is called Return on Capital Employed (ROCE) and is defined as:

$$\frac{\text{Operating profit before interest} \times 100}{\text{Capital employed}}$$

 **brilliant** definition

Capital employed is the amount of money (capital) which is invested (employed) in a business. It can be calculated from the balance sheet as total equity plus non-current liabilities or total assets (current and non-current) less current liabilities.

There is a potential problem with the ROCE, which is what capital employed figure to use in the calculation. Normally, the year-end figure is used, but might be higher than the capital employed at the beginning of the year. Some companies use a simple average figure, taking the average of the capital employed at the start and end of the year. Others use a rolling average, which might be best in a highly seasonal business. Whatever capital employed figure is used is a matter of judgement for the business. The important thing is to be consistent from one year to another with the calculations.

## brilliant tip

To ensure that all financial ratios are comparable, any calculations must be consistent over time. Slightly different calculations from those given in this chapter can be used provided they are consistent over time.

The ROCE tells us the return made on capital employed before any distributions of profits (e.g. taxation, dividends or interest). For Systera, the ROCE was 21.09% in 2009 and 21.44% in 2010. This is quite a good return and is well above any interest available on deposits. It is thus a rate of return which might compensate investors for the additional risk. Many companies also compare their ROCE with that of similar companies to see if they are making a comparable return. A variant of the ROCE is the Return on Shareholders Funds which shows the return on share capital only (see Figure 10.2).

To help explain the nature of the return made by Systera, it is possible to break the ROCE into two components, which are called (1) profit margin and (2) asset turnover. These two components isolate how the capital of the business generates profits. Capital is used to buy assets, which in turn generate sales, and sales subsequently generate profit. This raises two questions: (1) how profitable are sales, and (2) how well is capital used to generate those sales? The first question is answered by the profit margin ratio, the second by the asset turnover. Each is calculated as follows:

$$\text{Profit margin} = \frac{\text{operating profit before interest} \times 100}{\text{sales}}$$

$$\text{Asset turnover} = \frac{\text{sales}}{\text{capital employed}}$$

The profit margin (often called return on sales) tells us how profitable every pound of sales was. For Systera, you can see the profit margin increased from 35.06% to 40.42% year-on-year. This improved profit-ability is a good sign. Changes in the profit margin are caused by either increases/decreases in sales price and/or lower/higher costs. To find out the exact reason(s), we would need more detailed information than that presented in the financial statements. Again, the trend of the profit margin over a longer period of time, and comparisons against other companies, in the same business sector might be useful.

The asset turnover tells us how well capital employed is being used to generate sales. It is normally expressed as a multiple of capital employed. Some companies may have high capital employed, others not, depending on for example whether the business is more equipment or labour intensive. Looking at Systera, the asset turnover is less than one each year, meaning that capital employed does not generate its own value in sales, and in fact falls from 0.6 to 0.53 year on year. A low asset turnover is not necessarily a bad thing, as it may be compensated for by a high profit margin; this seems to be the case for Systera. But what might have caused the decrease from 2009 to 2010? We can't tell from the ratio itself. However, looking at the balance sheet, we can see that the value of non-current assets increased by almost £235,000. It is possible that new plant or equipment has been purchased and this has not yet realised its full efficiency.

## brilliant tip

Above, I have guessed that asset turnover may have declined as new equipment may not yet be fully productive. This is only a guess and would need to be verified. As you read this chapter, I'll offer possible interpretations for changes in ratios. These interpretations, while being reasonable, may not be correct. If you are analysing your own financial statements, you'll know your business circumstances and will be able to give more definite interpretations. If it's another business you cannot be so sure and might need to dig deeper.

If you are mathematically minded, you might notice that the profit margin multiplied by the asset turnover gives the ROCE. For example, for Systera in 2009 this is 35.06% × 0.602, which equals 21.09% (taking account of the small discrepancy owing to rounding).

You can calculate more profitability ratios to get more detail on the nature of profits. One very common ratio is the gross profit margin, which is calculated as follows:

$$\frac{\text{Gross profit} \times 100}{\text{Sales}}$$

The gross profit margin reflects the profitability of a business based on the costs of purchase or manufacture versus sales, i.e. gross profit (see Chapter 4). In general, a particular business sector will have an average gross profit margin. For example, the margin in a restaurant might be quite high while a motor dealer typically works on a small margin. For Systera, you can see the gross profit margin has increased from 54.9% to 59.5%. Therefore, linking back to the profit margin component of the ROCE, we can say that the increase in profit margin can in part be attributed to a better gross profit margin. This in turn means that either the selling prices were better than previous and/or purchase/manufacture costs were lower.

Ratios for expenditure items could also be calculated. I don't do any here, but you could calculate each expense as a percentage of sales. This might help you find the root causes of increases in cost. For example, if you calculate distribution costs as a percentage of sales, you can determine how efficient your distribution is. If you get more sales out of the same distribution costs, your distribution channels are operating more effectively.

## Analysing efficiency, liquidity and solvency

In calculating the ROCE above you've learned how to measure the efficiency of assets in a business. Now let's do a more detailed analysis of the current assets of a business. We can calculate ratios to assess how well inventory, trade receivables and trade payables are being managed. In addition, cash is a very important current asset and you've learned in Chapter 9 how important it is to budget for the cash requirements of a business. A business needs to ensure that its working capital (current assets less current liabilities) is managed correctly to ensure too much cash is not tied-up in inventory or trade receivables and cash is available to pay suppliers. Therefore, how well the elements of working capital are managed is important in determining the solvency and liquidity of a business.

> ### brilliant definition
>
> **Liquidity** refers to the ability to convert assets to cash. For example, inventories may be more liquid (i.e. can be sold for cash more quickly) than a non-current asset like a building.
>
> **Solvency** refers to the ability of a business to pay debts as they fall due.

Liquidity and solvency are closely related concepts. If assets cannot be converted to cash, debts like loan repayments or payments to suppliers may not be met. To be unable to pay debts as they fall due means a business is insolvent, which quite often leads to failure of the business. If the components of working capital are well managed, then solvency issues should not arise. Let's now calculate a number of ratios which help determine how well working capital is managed.

## Working capital management ratios

We can calculate a ratio for each of inventory, trade receivables and trade payables which help interpret how well working capital is managed. The first ratio is inventory turnover, which is calculated as follows:

$$\text{Inventory turnover} = \frac{\text{cost of sales}}{\text{average inventory}}$$

This ratio tells us how many times a year inventory is sold. You'll notice the bottom line (denominator) says 'average inventory', which might be a simple average of the inventory at the start of the year and the end of the year, or a rolling average. The reason for using an average is to try to remove seasonal variations.

Looking back at Systera, the inventory turnover has remained relatively stable year-on-year at 4.4 and 4.2 times. Put another way, inventory remains in the business for 86 days on average in 2010 (365 days per annum divided by 4.2 times). I have used the average inventory values for each year, which I have calculated as the average of the opening and closing stock figures as given in the income statement. For example, the 2009 figure is £44,800 (47,000 + 42,600 / 2).

A downward trend in the inventory turnover figure may be an indicator of poor inventory control. For example, a store or warehouse may be poorly organised or older stock not sold. Again, we cannot say this for certain from the figures but at least we can ask the question. Inventory turnover depends to a large extent on the type of business. For example, if I look at the 2009 financial statements of a retailer like Sainsbury (http://www.jsainsburys.co.uk), I get the following data:

|  | £m |
| --- | --- |
| Cost of sales | 17,875 |
| Inventory | 689 |

This gives an inventory turnover of 26 times per year, or on average, inventory is held for 14 days. This makes sense as Sainsbury's main business is in fast-moving consumer goods (FMCG). In comparison, if I look at the 2009 financial statements of Siemens, the global electronic and engineering company (http://www.siemens.com), I get the following data:

|  | €m |
| --- | --- |
| Cost of sales | 55,941 |
| Inventory | 14,129 |

This gives an inventory turnover of 3.96 times per year or, on average, inventory is held for 92.2 days (365/3.96). While Siemens do make some FMCG products, the majority of their business is in the provision of technologies for automation, transportation and industry. Such products do not sell as fast as other consumer products. This example again highlights the need to be careful when comparing two businesses using ratio analysis. To compare Sainsbury with Tesco or Morrisons would make more sense.

The next ratio reflects how well trade receivables are managed:

$$\text{Average period of credit given} = \frac{\text{trade receivables} \times 365}{\text{credit sales}}$$

This ratio tells how many days credit, on average, is given to customers. The top line (numerator) is multiplied by 365 to give the answer in days. If you want it in months, multiply by 12 instead. Looking at Systera, the period of credit given has fallen from just over 50 days to 46 days. This may be a reflection of improved credit control within the business. The trend of this ratio is important. If the average period of credit is increasing, solvency may be affected as cash may not be available quickly enough to pay suppliers and other debts. If the trend is decreasing this may seem a good thing, but sales might be lost if credit control is too strict. It may also be possible to compare the ratio with an industry average. The period of credit given might vary too with the economic climate, with the period likely to be longer in tough times. In the UK, the average period of credit given is likely to be in the 45–60 day range.

Now let's see the average period of credit taken. This is very like the previous one, except it relates to suppliers. It is calculated as follows:

$$\text{Average period of credit taken} = \frac{\text{trade payables} \times 365}{\text{credit purchases}}$$

One thing to note about this ratio is that it may not always be possible to obtain the credit purchases figure from published financial statements.

## brilliant tip

If some figures are not available from published financial statements, a substitute figure may be used. For example, cost of sales may be used as a substitute for credit purchases. When substitute figures are used, be consistent with the figure and recognise that resulting calculations may not be as useful.

For Systera, the credit purchases figure is available. The average period of credit taken has increased quite a bit from 97 days to 116 days. Why is this you might ask? The other two working capital ratios (inventory turnover and days credit given) have remained relatively stable, meaning that cash should be readily available. It may be that Systera is holding on to cash for longer, or has it bought something that has increased the monies owed to suppliers – like new equipment, which we noted earlier. This increase in average days credit taken may be a one-off blip, but again the trend over a longer time frame will tell a more accurate story. While most businesses do take credit, an increase in the period taken can be an indication of a liquidity problem. To determine if this is so, you should look at the inventory turnover and average period of credit given to see if the trend in these ratios is reflective of a potential problem. This highlights a key proviso of using ratios to analyse financial statements. That is, you should view ratios as inter-related and you need numerous ratios to give the full story.

All three of the ratios mentioned can be combined to give what is termed the 'cash conversion cycle'. This is the days in inventory (which is derived from inventory turnover), plus days credit given, minus days credit taken, as shown in Figure 10.3.

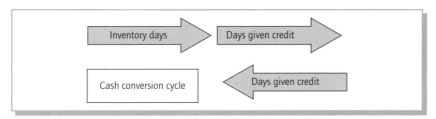

Figure 10.3 The cash conversion cycle

For Systera, the cash conversion cycle for 2010 is 16 days (86 + 46 − 116), which is quite good but obviously aided by the extended days credit taken. For 2009, the figure is 36 days (83 + 50 − 97). Thus, it could be argued that management at Systera may have deliberately negotiated longer credit terms to help the cash conversion cycle. Without a detailed breakdown of the amounts owed, we cannot know for sure. Again, the trend in the cash conversion cycle over time is important. If it is getting longer, it may be reflective of underlying management problems.

## Solvency ratios

There are two ratios commonly used to assess whether a business may have liquidity and/or solvency problems. The first one is called the current ratio, which is calculated as follows:

$$\text{Current ratio} = \frac{\text{current assets}}{\text{current liabilities}}$$

The basic concept of this ratio is that for a company to be able to pay its debts as they fall due, current assets should cover current liabilities by a multiple. For Systera, the ratio has dis-improved from 2009 to 2010, from 2.49:1 to 2.12:1. Generally a current ratio of at least 2:1 is good. This means that current assets are twice current liabilities. So, even if some stock could not be sold or some trade receivables not paid, current liabilities would still be covered for payment. However, the 2:1 figure is only a guideline.

 **brilliant** tip

Any ratios which have suggested 'yardsticks' need to be taken in context. For example, the current ratio has a suggested yardstick of 2:1, or the ROCE is often suggested as 15% or better. However, such measures do need to take into account the nature of a business.

For example, the current ratio of Sainsbury from their 2009 financial statements works out at 0.54:1, which is well below the 2:1 yardstick. This is not a problem as businesses like Sainsbury tend to have low inventory, low receivables and high trade payables.

The second ratio used to assess liquidity/solvency is the liquid ratio, and it is calculated as follows:

$$\text{Liquid ratio} = \frac{\text{current assets} - \text{inventory}}{\text{current liabilities}}$$

This ratio is also called the *quick ratio* or the *acid test ratio*. It is very similar to the current ratio, except that inventory is deducted from current assets. This is because inventory is traditionally regarded as being the least liquid current asset. For Systera, the liquid ratio has also declined, from 1.84:1 to 1.49:1. A generally accepted yardstick for the liquid ratio is at least 1:1, meaning that cash and trade receivables should equal current liabilities. Again, this yardstick needs to be treated with some caution and the industry/sector should be considered. Using the Sainsbury 2009 financial statements, the liquid ratio works out at 0.30:1, which might lead one to conclude that the company has liquidity problems. As an exercise, why not calculate the current and liquid ratios for other companies like Sainsbury (e.g. Tesco or Morrisons).

The current and liquid ratios serve as useful indicators of the liquidity/ solvency of a business. However, as with other ratios, the trend over time is important. Any business may face short-term liquidity problems which could skew either of the above ratios. Short-term liquidity problems may arise as customers are slow to pay or inventories remain unsold. Such problems are normally overcome through focused management of inventory and receivables.

## Analysing gearing and investment

The final ratios we'll examine are of interest to investors and lenders. While all ratios you've learned so far are also important for providers of capital, there are several more focused ratios which are particularly useful for this group.

First, let's look at two ratios which are particularly useful to lenders like banks. A bank will be interested in two things: how much existing debt does a business have and can repayments be made? The former can be assessed by the debt/equity ratio, the latter by the interest cover ratio.

The debt/equity ratio is calculated as follows:

$$\text{Debt/equity ratio} = \frac{\text{debt}}{\text{equity}}$$

Debt in this case means long-term debt, which is normally taken to mean long-term bank loans and other debt finance found under the non-current liabilities heading in the balance sheet. Equity is the shareholders' equity, or the capital provided by or attributable to shareholders (share capital and accumulated profits). For Systera, the debt/equity ratio has improved from 0.16:1 to 0.12:1 (or 16% to 12%). If you look at the balance sheet, you can see that this improvement is due to the increased equity as the debt level does not change. In general, if this ratio is greater than 1:1 (i.e. debt is greater than equity), then a business is said to be highly-geared; less than 1:1 makes it a low-geared business.

For a potential investor or lender, the higher the level of gearing the more risky the business may be. From a potential shareholder's view, if more cash is needed to pay interest on debt, less cash is available to pay dividends. From a lender's view, if the level of existing debt is high, repaying any additional debt may be problematic. However, high gearing is not necessarily a bad thing. Once monies borrowed are put to good use and earn a return greater than the rate of interest paid, overall profits should grow which in turn can be used to pay interest, dividends and loan repayments.

The next ratio, interest cover, is useful to lenders in particular. It is calculated as follows:

$$\text{Interest cover} = \frac{\text{operating profit}}{\text{interest}}$$

The interest cover ratio simply tells us how many times operating profit (which is before interest, tax and dividends) covers interest. From a lender's perspective, a higher level of interest cover is preferred. If the interest cover is low, then a business might have trouble meeting interest payment on borrowings, which certainly would not bode well for repayments of the principal (the amount borrowed). Looking at Systera, you can see that interest cover is quite good in both years at 13.5 and 17.2 times. This, combined with the low gearing above, would be good news for any potential lender.

While lenders are concerned with ensuring the interest and principal are repaid, shareholders are in a similar way concerned with the ability of a business to generate profits so that dividends can be paid. Even if dividends paid are not a very high proportion of profits, shareholders may be able to sell their shares at a profit. Having said that, unless a company can show a history of good profits and sound plans for the future, share value is unlikely to increase. Thus, shareholders are concerned with both profitability and dividends. While ratios like the ROCE may be useful to shareholders, there are a number of other ratios which they may find particularly useful.

Earnings per share (EPS) represents the profit per individual share. It as calculated as follows:

$$\text{EPS} = \frac{\text{profit after tax, interest and preference dividends}}{\text{number of ordinary shares in issue}}$$

The top portion of the EPS ratio represents the profit that is available for paying out as a dividend. This does not mean it will be paid out, but it is the profit in theory available to ordinary shareholders. Given that the bottom portion of the EPS is the number of ordinary shares issued, the EPS is not very comparable between two companies. However, the trend of the EPS of a particular company is an important indicator of how well the company is performing and it is also an important variable in determining a shares price (see the price/earnings ratio next).

For Systera, we can see that EPS has fallen from £1.07 per share to 86p per share. Can you see why? Jot down your answer:

While earnings for Systera have increased somewhat, the number of shares in issue has risen from 119,200 to 191,900 also. This means that the EPS will be lower. This highlights a potential problem with the EPS ratio in that the number of shares issued may vary from year to year. In practice, this is overcome by using a weighted average number of shares in issue over a year. This evens out the effect of new share issues.

The price/earnings (P/E) ratio shows a company's current share price relative to its current earnings – which assumes the share is traded on a stock exchange, i.e. the company is a public company. It is calculated as follows:

$$\text{P/E ratio} = \frac{\text{market price per share}}{\text{earning per share}}$$

Looking at Systera, the P/E ratio has increased to 10.23 from 6.04. In general, a high P/E suggests that investors are expecting higher earnings growth in the future compared to companies with a lower P/E. However, the P/E ratio doesn't tell the whole story. It's usually more useful to compare the P/E ratios of one company to other companies in the same industry, to the market in general, or against the company's own P/E trend. It would not be useful for investors to compare the P/E of a tech-nology company (high P/E) to a utility company (low P/E) since each industry has very different growth prospects. Care should be taken with the P/E ratio because the bottom part of the ratio is the EPS which, as stated above, may not be that comparable between companies. There are some crude yardsticks for the P/E ratio as follows:

- A P/E of less than 5 to 10 means that company is viewed as not performing so well.
- A ratio of 10 to 15 means a company is performing satisfactorily.
- A ratio above 15 means that the future prospects for a company are extremely good.

Again, as with all such yardsticks, these will vary by industry and depend on other factors which drive share price, e.g. bad publicity or the general economic outlook. We will come across the P/E ratio again in Chapter 11.

To sum up, you now know about some financial ratios which can be used to assess the profitability, liquidity, solvency, efficiency and capital structure of an organisation. You now know that financial statements, while useful and informative, are not usually directly comparable. Financial ratios overcome this problem. Analysing a business using ratios does have limitations which I have outlined. However, by analysing an organisation through a combination of financial statements and financial ratios, a lender, investor or supplier will obtain a reasonable picture of how a company is performing and whether it is managing its resources efficiently.

 **brilliant** recap

- Financial statements are limited, as the figures therein may not be directly comparable with those of other companies.

- Financial ratios can be used to overcome this limitation and provide a better picture of the performance of a business.

- Ratios can be calculated to assess profitability, efficiency, solvency, gearing and investment return.

- You need to consider a number of ratios under each category to form a view on the business.

- Yardsticks provided for some financial ratios need to be treated with care.

**CHAPTER 11**

# Using financial
# statements to
# value a business

N ow that you know the basics of book-keeping, financial statement preparation and some planning techniques, things should
run relatively smoothly for you. Sometimes when a business is
up and running and doing well, it might expand by seeking out a business
to purchase.

Why not invest your assets in the companies you really like? As
Mae West said, 'Too much of a good thing can be wonderful.'

*Warren Buffett*

Buying a business is a big decision. Even if you like the business you want
to buy, many factors need to be considered: the location, market, cost
structure, existing management and product portfolio, to name a few.
But, an important factor is the price you pay. Pay too much and future
returns may not justify the cost; pay too little and you may find some skel-
etons in the cupboard. In this chapter, you'll learn some basic guidelines
about how businesses can be valued. This gives you the basic knowledge
to assess if the price is right. I will use some of the points you learned in
Chapter 10, so flick back if you need to.

## Valuation basics

As you know from Chapter 5, the balance sheet of a business is a list of
its assets and liabilities. Put another way, the balance sheet represents the
value of a business. However, the value as depicted in the balance sheet is
a historic value and does not reflect the future profits of a business. This
historic value is referred to as the 'book value' of a business as it is the

money value recorded in the books of account. For example, looking back at the balance sheet of Systera plc in Chapter 10 (see p. 176), the book value of the business for 2010 is £843,600 – which is the book value of equity.

If you were to sell your business you'd ask for a price above the book value if you could. There may be many valid reasons for this, such as:

- Some assets of the business, such as land and buildings, may not be reflected in the balance sheet at their true market value.
- You may want to be compensated for loss of future earnings.
- You may have built up a loyal customer base over time, for which you want to be compensated.

If a business is a public limited company, valuing it is relatively simple as you could use the market price of a share as a guideline. Without being too detailed here, the price of any shares sold publically should incorporate all available information on a business. Thus, if it is expected that a company will continue to be profitable, the market price of the share is likely to be higher than any book value. The term 'market capitalisation' is used to describe the total market value of a public company. It can be calculated as follows:

Market price per share × number of shares in issue

Obviously, the market price can move up and down, drastically affecting the market value. Think of the declining market share price of many UK and global banks in 2008 and 2009.

If the company is private, things are a little more difficult as shares are not traded on any market. This does not mean that it is impossible to put a 'market value' on share of a private company. In Chapter 10 (see p. 177), we calculated the ROCE for Systera plc in 2010 at 21.44%. Let's assume Systera is a private company. A potential investor or buyer of this business might say this is an extremely good return, and take 21% as a good return on investment. What this investor is effectively saying is:

$$21\% = \frac{\text{profit before interest and tax}}{\text{market value}}$$

Plugging in the figures from Systera for 2010, we can calculate the market value as:

$$\text{Market value} = \frac{202,600}{21\%} \quad \text{(i.e. } 190,800 + 11,800)$$

This gives a value of £964,762. Dividing this by the number of shares (191,900) would give a value of £5.03 per share. This is a rough approximation of how to value shares in a private company, but the value would be affected by the return an investor wants. Let's now look at some techniques used to value businesses.

## Valuation techniques

Business valuation techniques fall into a number of categories, depending on their focus:

- business assets
- historical earnings or cash flow
- a combination of assets and earnings
- the market for similar businesses, including comparable sales, industry rule of thumb, and P/E ratio methods
- future earnings.

I'll explain each below, assuming in all cases that the business to be valued is a private company.

## Asset-based valuations

You've already learned the concept of book value of a business. You can think of this as the minimum value price a business might be sold at. This may not be the case, though, as the liquidation value of a business may be lower. Liquidation value is the amount that would be left over if a business is sold quickly, without taking the time to get the full market value, and then using the proceeds to pay off all debts. There's little point in going through all the trouble of negotiating a sale of a business if it's sold for a liquidation value – it would be easier to go out of business, and save the time and costs involved in selling the business. Thus, liquidation value is not generally considered at all, although it might be a floor price which could be used in negotiations.

**brilliant tip**

Book value, while a better reflection of the value of a business than liquidation value, should be treated with some caution. A business owner might 'dress-up' the financial statements before showing them to a potential buyer. This does not mean that something illegal is taking place, rather the seller is trying to reflect what the financial statements might look like under a new owner. For example, in a family run business, salaries of family members might be excluded from income statements or profit forecasts.

## Earnings or cash flow based valuations

An earnings method has been shown earlier and this is commonly used. It involves first determining a figure that represents the historical earnings (profits) of the company. This might be an average of the operating profits before interest and tax over previous years.

**brilliant example**

If the operating profit before interest and tax of a business was £200,000 and the buyer required a return of 25%, an earnings method would yield a price of £200,000/0.25 or £800,000.

An alternative to profits is to use cash flows. The free cash flow of a business can be used as a starting point, which can be taken as the net increase in cash from the cash flow statement and adding back any interest paid. The resulting figure is the cash the business would have if debt-free. Then, assuming the buyer of the business borrows money to complete the purchase, it is possible to determine the value of the business incorporating the buyer's expected return. Have a look at the brilliant example below.

 **example**

A business has free cash flows of £80,000 per year. A buyer is willing to buy this business using borrowings which will be repaid in five years. This requires a minimum free cash flow of 5 × £80,000 = £400,000.

Now, assume the buyer requires a 20% annual return = £80,000 × 20% = £16,000 meaning that only £64,000 per year is available to make loan repayments. An annual payment of £64,000 could support a five-year loan of approximately £277,086 at 5% interest, or £242,610 at 10% interest. These are effectively the business values.

(You can easily find a calculator for these types of calculation using a Google search.)

## Combined asset and earnings valuations

As you know about assets and earnings valuation methods already, here's an example of a combined assets and earnings method.

 **example**

Let's say the book value of a business as per the balance sheet is £280,000. This is a minimum or base price. Now let's assume that your historical annual earnings figure is £150,000. How much of this earnings figure is attributable to the assets? Let's assume the ROCE is calculated at 10% currently. Thus, earnings attributable to assets is £15,000. Subtracting this 'asset return' figure from your total earnings gives what is often termed 'excess earnings': £150,000 − £15,000 = £135,000.

Now suppose the required return from the business is 20%. Using the excess earnings as a base for this return, the value of excess earnings is £675,000 (£135,000/20%). Add to this the book value of your assets, and you arrive at a total price of £955,000 (£280,000 + £675,000).

The 'excess earnings' method shown above is common in practice. A variant is to revalue balance sheet assets at current market value, which will put a higher value on the business.

## Valuations based on similar businesses

You could value a business based on the market price of similar businesses at a point in time. They might provide a good benchmark value and compared to the methods you've seen thus far, a market-based method is a good reality check.

A comparable sale method attempts to use similar businesses that have recently been sold as a basis for valuation. It may be possible to use the comparable sales figures to set a price for your business, adjusting appropriately for differences. While this idea is readily applicable to property sales, the method may be difficult to apply to business valuations because of problems in gathering information about business sales and because of the unique character of each business.

Rules of thumb/industry averages are another frequently used method. These are based on experience and on published data for a particular industry. For example, the type of business you might want to buy has been selling for about four times annual revenue. However, a rule of thumb does not take into account any of the factors that make a business unique. Nevertheless, small businesses in particular are often sold at a price based on rule of thumb, simply because it's a relatively fast and simple method, and because it will result in a price that seems reasonable based on sales of similar businesses.

In Chapter 10, you learned about the P/E ratio. P/E ratios of public companies or an industry are widely available – for example on the Financial Times website (http://www.ft.com). The P/E ratio of a public company can be a useful comparative measure to value a similar private company. However, private companies are possibly more risky than a public company and can command a premium price. Also, if you buy a private company, it may be much harder to liquidate (sell) it than selling shares in a public company. For these reasons, using the P/E ratio of a public company to value a private company should be treated with some caution.

## Valuation on future earnings

Theoretically, anyone purchasing a business is more interested in the future of the business than the past. Therefore, a valuation based on the company's expected future earnings, discounted back to the value of money in today's terms, should be very close to answering the question about how much the business is really worth.

At least that's the theory. In practice, valuations based on future performance of the company are probably the most difficult to do because we must make estimates and projections of what is likely to happen in the future. Nevertheless, it may be worth trying one of these methods. If carefully done, valuation methods based on future earnings can result in setting the highest reasonable price for a business.

Methods based on future earnings are frequently used by large organisations in merger or acquisition situations. So, how do you go about setting a price based on future earnings? The first step is to look at the financial statements. Working from these, you can create projected statements that extend for five or more years into the future. Each year's free cash flows or earnings can be determined, as seen above. These projections should assume no major changes by a prospective buyer, since you are trying to value the company as it exists today.

Once this is done, the projected free cash flow (or earnings) from each year is discounted back to the present value of money, to arrive at what is called the net present value (NPV) of each cash flow. These NPVs are added up, to arrive at a total NPV of the company's earnings for the projected future. How do you compute NPV? The easiest way is to look up what is called a present value table (search Google for 'present value table'). Below is an extract from a present value table.

| Year | 9.0% | 9.5% | 10.0% | 10.5% |
|------|------|------|-------|-------|
| 1 | 0.917 | 0.913 | 0.909 | 0.905 |
| 2 | 0.842 | 0.834 | 0.826 | 0.819 |
| 3 | 0.772 | 0.762 | 0.751 | 0.741 |

The above present value table is read by looking at the year in which the cash flow occurs and the presumed rate of interest, or 'discount rate'. For example, a cash flow of £1,000 in three years from now would be equivalent to £751 today if the discount rate is 10% (£1,000 × 0.751). The key question is deciding which discount rate to use. The higher the rate, the lower the present value. The discount rate must reflect a best guess as to what the market rate will be for investments of a similar nature over the next five years or more. It could also factor in a buyer's expected cost of capital (i.e. the interest rate paid on borrowings to buy the business). If you need to, seek professional investment appraisal advice from an accountant or financial adviser on which discount rate to use.

 **brilliant** example

Let's say that after doing your best to look into the future and you forecast the next three years' cash flows as below. Assuming a 10% discount rate, the present value figures are as shown.

| Year | | Cash flow | Discount factor | Present value |
|---|---|---|---|---|
| | 1 | 100,000 | 0.909 | 90,900 |
| | 1 | 150,000 | 0.826 | 123,900 |
| | 1 | 180,000 | 0.751 | 135,180 |
| | | | | 349,980 |

Figure 11.1 Present value figures

Adding up the present values gives a net present value of £349,980, which is what the cash flows are worth today. Now let's assume that the total value of net assets at the end of year 3 will be £1,000,000. This equates to £751,000 in today's terms (£1,000,000 × 0.751). Therefore, we can say the value of the business using this method is £751,000 + £349,980, which is £1,100,980. This method is a combination of assets and earnings (cash flows) but with the added benefit of bringing future projections back to today's money value.

The NPV method is often cited as the most 'technically' sound method of evaluating future cash flows and therefore is used frequently. However, its biggest problem can be identifying and/or estimating those same cash flows. In the example above, I have equated cash flows to profits, but as you know from Chapter 7, cash flows and profits are not the same. Cash flows are less subjective and this is why it is better to use them in present value calculations where possible.

## brilliant recap

- Financial statements portray the book value of a company, which may not be the same as market value.

- The market value of a public company can be determined by reference to its share price and the number of shares in issue.

- The valuation of a private company is more difficult. A value can be derived using the book value of assets as a starting point and then future cash flows and earnings can be examined.

- Other valuation methods are possible, using comparisons to similar companies for which market data is available.

- The present value of future cash flows and assets using the NPV technique is probably the most technically sound method of valuing a business.

# CHAPTER 12

# Getting ready for an audit

W e've covered the main book-keeping and accounting tasks, and this final chapter looks at what you need to do if and when the accounts of your business are subject to inspection by external person(s). From what you have learned, you should be well on the way to ensuring that the work you've done is of a reasonable standard.

In general, the accounting records of a business will be checked at least annually by an accountant or auditor. If a business is a sole trader, then it is possible that an accountant prepares the financial statements at year-end only. This may also be the case for smaller companies, whereas larger companies will most probably have internal accountants and also engage external auditors to verify the financial statements. The role of an auditor has already been mentioned in Chapter 6. It is also possible that a business is subject to an audit by the tax authorities such as HM Revenue and Customs (HMRC). An audit by HMRC is possible for any of the taxes a business is registered for (e.g. VAT, PAYE, etc.), or there could be a full audit of all taxes.

Most businesses get really worried when they receive notification of a tax audit, but usually there's not a lot to worry about. This is because if you follow good book-keeping and accounting practices and the additional advice given in this chapter, the chance of getting an audit are quite low – maybe once in the lifetime of a business owner/manager. If, on the other hand, you don't, then alarm bells may be set off which trigger an audit and these tend to be much more focused and typically find something incorrectly treated in the accounts or records.

For the rest of this chapter we'll focus on what you should do if you get selected for an audit by the tax authorities. Not all tasks in preparing for an audit are the responsibility of a book-keeper or accountant, but at the end of the day remember that all accounting comes back to the recording of daily transactions in the day books. Of course, the points made are equally relevant to preparing for the annual visit by external auditors. Some additional tasks you might need to do for these auditors are mentioned towards the end of the chapter.

## What is a tax audit?

All businesses register for and pay taxes like VAT, Pay-As-You-Earn (PAYE), income tax or corporation tax. While beyond the scope of this book, income tax refers to tax on income which is non-PAYE. For example, the profit made by a sole trader is subject to income tax in the same way that a job is subject to PAYE taxes. Corporation tax is paid on company profits.

In simple terms, a tax audit is a cross-check of the information and figures shown by a business in its tax returns against those shown in the business records. Thus, the basic aim of a tax audit is to ensure that the day books and other records are accurate, and the amounts reported to and paid over to the tax authorities are based on these records.

Normally, a single tax inspector or official will conduct an audit at a business premises. More staff may be involved if the size of the business merits it. You'll be informed in advance of the date of the audit, which can be changed if it does not suit. You'll also be informed of what taxes the audit will examine. In smaller businesses, the audit may also examine the personal tax affairs of the owner(s). Remember that the business entity concept (see Chapter 1) means that personal and business affairs are separate. For example, a partnership might be audited, with the tax affairs of each partner as an individual also subject to audit.

Typically, businesses are selected for a tax audit using one of the following three selection criteria.

### Screening tax returns

The vast majority of audits are selected using some form of screening process. Screening involves examining the tax returns made and reviewing compliance history – compliance means filing returns on time and paying taxes when due. Figures on the tax returns are analysed in the light of trends and patterns in the particular business or sector.

## Projects on business sectors

From time to time, projects are conducted to examine tax compliance levels in particular business sectors. The returns for a large number of businesses in a particular sector are screened in detail and a proportion of these are selected for audit. For example, many independent contractors have been the focus of audits from HMRC in recent years. The focus of these audits is to establish if these individuals are in fact employees rather than contractors, and should be in the PAYE system.

## Random selection

This is in addition to the two methods mentioned above. It means that all businesses have a possibility of being audited. A very small proportion, less than 5%, of audits are selected using this method.

# Preparing for a tax audit

You learned in Chapter 2 that you should invoice customers without delay to avoid giving any extra credit. If you do this, your sales day book and associated ledgers should always be up-to-date. This applies for all other business transactions too, so you should always have an up-to-date set of records. This is the starting point for any tax audit. If records are not fully up-to-date, you need to get things in order as soon as possible.

**brilliant** tip

One sure way to keep up-to-date is to do a bank reconciliation each month when you receive the bank statements (see Chapter 2). You'll need to have all records in order before you can do this, so it forces you to keep your books in a timely fashion.

Assuming your records are in order, the next step is to get yourself prepared for the day of the audit. The best thing to do is take out the relevant records and have them ready in a separate file for the tax inspector. You will have been informed of the tax/taxes to be audited and the period of time. So, for example, if the audit covers PAYE records for 2009 and 2010, have these ready. Remember too, that the records might include other day books or computer reports you might not think of in the first instance. For example, in a PAYE audit the cheque payments book and the petty cash book might be checked to see if payments were made to employees that were not recorded in the payroll records.

The next step you should do is a general review of the business. While an audit may focus on a specific tax, sometimes it can lead to a much broader examination of the accounting records and/or the tax affairs of the business owner(s).

 **example**

If an audit of PAYE taxes is undertaken, then the full payroll records will be made available to the tax inspectors. For example, if the wages or drawings of the business owners were low, this might prompt an inspector to look further for 'undeclared' income. This would broaden the scope from PAYE to income tax and possibly also to VAT if the undeclared income was in fact cash sales which were unrecorded.

Some things to think about in doing a general review of the business include:

- Is the turnover (i.e. sales) of the business reflective of the underlying profits the business makes?
- Are all cash receipts recorded and banked? In other words, particularly in a cash business ensure that the cash recorded as passing through the cash registers is accounted for by means of a cash book showing any payments out before cash is lodged.
- Do a quick sum of the sales and purchases you have reported on VAT returns. Compare these totals with your sales and purchases day book totals (or the totals from you accounting software); they should be the same.
- In sole trader or partnership, are drawings adequate for the lifestyle of the owner/partners?

- Are all expenditures vouched for? In other words, are all expenses related back to a proper source document, e.g. a purchase invoice or receipt. Check the purchases day book and/or the cheque payments book to ensure all expenses are supported by an appropriate source document.
- Have any personal expenses being classified as business expenses?
- Are all wages paid adequate and reflective of the work done by employees? If not, this could suggest cash is being paid 'under the counter' to employees.

If you find anything wrong, don't try to cover it up. All book-keepers and accountants make mistakes and you'll often find these when combing back over the books. If the monetary value of any error is small, a tax inspector or external auditor will not be too worried. If on the other hand, there is a problem then the best thing to do is to be upfront and admit it. For example, let's assume you're a sole trader and haven't been recording all cash sales, instead keeping a sizeable portion for yourself. However, by doing this, the drawings figure is too low for the fact that you have mortgage, partner, two kids and two cars. Let's say you know you have not recorded £20,000 in cash sales in a year, and by putting this in the business the drawings figure would look much better. If you declare this £20,000 to the tax inspector, yes you will have to pay income tax due and possibly VAT too. But, more importantly you may avoid paying additional penalties and/or interest. HMRC and Ireland's Revenue Commissioners apply what I think is quite a fair approach to penalties. The approach taken depends on how 'bad' the taxpayer's behaviour has been. Here's what HMRC says:

Penalties are charged as a percentage of the extra tax due. The rate increases according to how bad a taxpayers' behaviour has been:

- No penalties apply if reasonable care has been taken.
- Up to 30% for careless behaviour.
- Up to 70% for deliberate mistakes.
- Up to 100% for deliberate and concealed mistakes.

You can read more about this at link http://www.hmrc.gov.uk. You can see how the approach leans much more heavily on businesses that deliberately conceal things. By the way, a 100% penalty means that any tax found to be due in the course of an audit is doubled. Interest for late payment might be added on top of this.

## Avoiding a tax audit

Having read this book you should be quite confident that you're on the way to keeping a 'clean' up-to-date set of books. Don't worry about making mistakes, as we all do. In addition to your good records, there are some further steps you can take to avoid been selected for a tax audit, as follows:

- Pay taxes and file returns on time. Use online filing if possible as this speeds things up and you may also get more time to pay taxes due.
- If there are unusual figures in any return made to tax authorities, why not take a little time to explain them. For example, sales and profit might fall due to increased competition, not because sales are unrecorded.
- Seek professional advice if you need to.

Keeping things tidy and timely is the best way to minimise the chances of a tax audit. It does not eliminate the possibility but, if selected, your business should be fine.

## Preparing for a visit by external auditors

An external auditor is a person(s), usually an accountant, who verifies financial statements of a limited company. External auditors do not always prepare financial statements, accountants do. Of course, an accountant can also be an external auditor and this is typically the case in smaller accounting practices.

In the UK, not all companies are required by law to have an auditor. Currently, if turnover is less than £6.5m and the balance sheet total is less that £3.26m, then no audit is required. This does not mean such companies won't have auditors as sometimes institutions like banks will insist on having 'audited' financial statements, meaning that an auditor verifies them as an accurate reflection of the underlying books of account. All other companies require an auditor to certify the financial statements as being accurate.

So what does an auditor actually do? Normally in a larger company, an accountant prepares monthly accounts for the managers of the business and at year-end, produces the financial statements as required by company law. Once the financial statements are done, the auditor then sets about doing checks and tests to ensure that the financial statements are accurate and represent fairly the underlying books of account. So, as business owner, accountant or book-keeper, the auditor will examine some of your work. Here are some of tests an auditor might do (it is by no means an exhaustive list):

● Conduct a 'walk-through' test. This means that the auditor takes a source document from beginning to end through the book-keeping and accounting system.

● Conduct a validity test. This means confirming that what is reflected in the accounting records or financial statements is real and actually exists.

● Undertake tests to ensure the completeness of the financial statements.

 **brilliant** definition

An **audit test** refers to activities conducted by an auditor to assess the accuracy of account balances and, in turn, financial statements.

As you might guess by the use of the word 'test', an auditor cannot examine all transactions. He or she will take a sample of transactions and use these as the basis for tests. There are of course risks associated with choosing a sample, the most obvious being that any sample transactions are not reflective of the majority. Auditors will select a sample number of transactions which will minimise the risk. The brilliant example below gives some practical details of the audit test types mentioned above.

 **example**

Here are some examples of audit tests.

1  Walk-through test. An auditor might want to test the sales processes. This would start with a sales order from a customer. The price charged on the invoice would be checked against that agreed on the sales order. The invoice would be traced to the sales day book and to the accounts receivable (sales) and nominal ledgers. Payment from the customer would also be traced through the cash receipts book, the ledgers and finally verified on the bank statement.

2  Validity test. The auditor might choose an asset from the balance sheet and check its physical location and condition. This is ensuring that the asset actually exists.

3  Completeness test. The auditor will send a letter to the business' bank branch asking for details of the balances on the business bank accounts at the end of the financial year. This not only verifies the bank balance, but also ensures that all bank accounts have in fact been revealed by the business.

As you can see from the audit tests described above, a business owner, accountant or book-keeper is likely to be asked to provide documentation to help the auditor complete the tests. Many businesses fear the annual visit by auditors. They view it as someone 'checking up' on them. Why not look at the visit in a positive light, as it provides external validation of any work you've done. You can then be reasonably sure you are doing a good job. In smaller companies where you do not have accountants internally, then it is likely an external accountant will both prepare and audit year-end financial statements (if required by company law).

**brilliant** recap

- A tax audit is when the tax authorities visit a business with the purpose of determining if the records of the business agree with information submitted on various tax returns.

- Tax audits tend to be focused, with some form of screening used to select the business for audit.

- The best preparation for a tax audit is a set of clean, well-organised accounting records.

- If you have something to tell the tax authorities, be upfront, as it can save you a lot of money in penalties.

- The best way to avoid a tax audit is to comply with dates for filing tax returns and paying taxes.

- External auditors may interact with book-keepers while conducting tests as part of the annual audit of a company.

# Glossary

**Absorption costing:** A method of calculating the cost of manufacturing a product or providing a service.

**Account:** A section in a ledger devoted to a single aspect of a business (e.g. a bank account, wages account, office expenses account).

**Accounting:** The recording, collating and communication of business data, usually of a monetary nature.

**Accounting cycle:** This covers everything from opening the books at the start of the year to closing them at the end. In other words, everything you need to do in one accounting year, accounting wise.

**Accounting equation:** The formula used to prepare a balance sheet: assets = liabilities + equity.

**Accounts payable:** An account in the nominal ledger which contains the overall balance of the purchase ledger.

**Accounts payable ledger:** A subsidiary ledger which holds the accounts of a business's suppliers. A single control account is held in the nominal ledger which shows the total balance of all the accounts in the purchase ledger.

**Accounts receivable:** An account in the nominal ledger which contains the overall balance of the sales ledger.

**Accounts receivable ledger:** A subsidiary ledger which holds the accounts of a business's customers. A single control account is held in the nominal ledger which shows the total balance of all the accounts in the sales ledger.

**Accruals:** If during the course of a business certain charges are incurred but no invoice is received then these charges are referred to as accruals (they 'accrue' or increase in value). A typical example is interest payable on a loan where you have not yet received a bank statement. These items (or an estimate of their value) should still be included in the income statement. When the real interest is received, an adjustment can be made to correct the estimate. Accruals can also apply to income.

**Accrual method of accounting:** Most businesses use the accrual method of accounting (because it is usually required by accounting regulations and the law). When you issue an invoice on credit (i.e. regardless of whether it is paid or not), it is treated as a taxable supply on the date it was issued for income tax purposes (or corporation tax for limited companies). The same applies to bills received from suppliers.

**Accumulated depreciation account:** This is an account held in the nominal ledger which holds the depreciation of a fixed asset until the end of the asset's useful life. It is credited each year with that year's depreciation, hence the balance increases (i.e. accumulates) over a period of time. Each asset will have its own accumulated depreciation account.

**Accumulated fund:** The surplus of income accumulated by a not-for-profit organisation over time.

**Arrears:** Bills which should have been paid. For example, if you have forgotten to pay your last three months' rent, then you are said to be three months in arrears on your rent.

**Assets:** Assets represent what a business owns or is due. Equipment, vehicles, buildings, creditors, money in the bank, cash are all examples of the assets of a business. Typical breakdown includes 'fixed assets', 'current assets' and 'non-current assets'. Fixed refers to equipment, buildings, plant, vehicles etc. Current refers to cash, money in the bank, debtors, etc. Non-current assets are the same as fixed assets.

**Associate company:** Within a group of companies, an associate is one where 20–50% of the ordinary shares are owned by the parent company.

**At cost:** The 'at cost' price usually refers to the price originally paid for something as opposed to, say, the retail price.

**Audit:** The process of checking every entry in a set of books to make sure they agree with the original paperwork (e.g. checking a journal's entries against the original purchase and sales invoices).

**Audit test:** Activities and tests conducted by an auditor to assess the accuracy of account balances and financial statements.

**Audit trail:** A list of transactions in the order they occurred. Most accounting software can readily provide an automatic audit trail report.

**Bad debts account:** An account in the nominal ledger to record the value of unrecoverable debts from customers. Real bad debts or those that are likely to happen can be deducted as expenses against tax liability (provided they refer specifically to a customer).

**Balance sheet:** A summary of all the accounts of a business. Usually prepared at the end of each financial year. The term 'balance sheet' implies that the combined balances of assets exactly equals the liabilities and equity.

**Bill:** A term typically used to describe a purchase invoice (e.g. an invoice from a supplier).

**Books of prime entry:** these record business transactions from source documents (like invoices or cheques). They may be a 'book' or more commonly, accounting software.

**Bought ledger:** See *purchase ledger*.

**Break-even:** The output level at which a business makes neither a profit nor a loss.

**Capital:** An amount of money put into the business (often by way of a loan) as opposed to money earned by the business.

**Capital employed:** The amount of money (capital) which is invested (employed) in a business. It can be calculated from the balance sheet as total equity plus non-current liabilities or total assets (current and non-current) less current liabilities.

**Capital assets:** See *non-current assets*.

**Cash accounting:** This term describes an accounting method whereby only invoices and bills which have been paid are accounted for. However, for most types of business in the UK, as far as the Inland Revenue are concerned, as soon as you issue an invoice (paid or not), it is treated as revenue and must be accounted for. An exception is VAT: Revenue &

Customs normally require you to account for VAT on an accrual basis, however there is an option called 'Cash Accounting' whereby only paid items are included as far as VAT is concerned (e.g. if most of your sales are on credit, you may benefit from this scheme: contact your local HMRC office for the current rules and turnover limits).

**Cash book:** A journal where cash sales and purchases are entered. A cash book can also be used to record the transactions of a bank account.

**Cash flow statement:** A financial statement that shows the changes in the cash balance of a business and analyses the sources and uses of cash.

**Cash in hand:** See *undeposited funds account.*

**Chart of accounts:** A list of all the accounts held in the nominal ledger.

**Compensating error:** A double-entry term applied to a mistake which has cancelled out another mistake.

**Contribution:** A term used in management accounting to describe selling price less all variable costs.

**Control account:** An account held in a ledger which summarises the balance of all the accounts in the same or another ledger. Typically each subsidiary ledger will have a control account which will be mirrored by another control account in the nominal ledger.

**Cook the books:** Falsify a set of accounts. See also *creative accounting.*

**Cost (in management accounting):** A monetary measure of resources sacrificed or forgone to achieve an objective.

**Cost (in relation to stocks/inventories):** The amount for which the items were bought, including delivery charges, customs duties, etc. (but not VAT).

**Cost accounting:** An area of management accounting which deals with the costs of a business in terms of enabling the management to manage the business more effectively.

**Cost of sales:** A formula for working out the direct costs of your sales (including stock) over a particular period. The result represents the gross profit. The formula is: opening stock + purchases + direct expenses =

closing stock. Also called cost of goods sold when goods are manufactured for resale, rather than bought.

**Creative accounting:** A questionable means of making a company's figures appear more (or less) appealing to shareholders, bankers, etc.

**Credit:** A column in a journal or ledger to record the 'from' side of a transaction (e.g. if you buy some petrol using a cheque then the money is paid from the bank to the petrol account, you would therefore credit the bank when making the journal entry).

**Credit note:** A sales invoice in reverse. A typical example is where you issue an invoice for £100, the customer then returns £25 worth of the goods, and so you issue the customer with a credit note to say that you owe the customer £25.

**Creditors:** A list of suppliers to whom the business owes money.

**Creditors control account:** An account in the nominal ledger which contains the overall balance of the purchase ledger.

**Current assets:** These include money in the bank, petty cash, money received but not yet banked (see 'cash in hand'), money owed to the business by its customers, raw materials for manufacturing, and stock bought for resale. They are termed 'current' because they are active accounts. Money flows in and out of them each financial year and we will need frequent reports of their balances if the business is to survive (e.g. 'Do we need more stock and have we got enough money in the bank to buy it?').

**Current liabilities:** These include bank overdrafts, short-term loans (less than a year), and what the business owes its suppliers. They are termed 'current' for the same reasons outlined under 'current assets' in the previous paragraph.

**Daybooks:** see *books of prime entry*.

**Debit:** A column in a journal or ledger to record the 'To' side of a transaction (e.g. if you are paying money into your bank account you would debit the bank when making the journal entry).

**Debtors:** A list of customers who owe money to the business.

**Debtors control account:** An account in the nominal ledger which contains the overall balance of the sales ledger.

**Depreciation:** The value of assets usually decreases as time goes by. The amount or percentage it decreases by is called depreciation. This is normally calculated at the end of every accounting period (usually a year) at a typical percentage rate of its last value. It is shown in both the profit and loss account and balance sheet of a business. See *straight-line depreciation*.

**Dividend:** The portion of profits paid to shareholders. There is no obligation on a company to pay a dividend.

**Direct cost:** A cost which can be specifically identified to a particular product or service.

**Double-entry book-keeping:** A system which accounts for every aspect of a transaction – where it came from and where it went to. This *from* and *to* aspect of a transaction (called crediting and debiting) is what the term double-entry means.

**Drawings:** The money taken out of a business by its owner(s) for personal use. This is entirely different to wages paid to a business's employees or the wages or remuneration of a limited company's directors (see *wages*).

**Entry:** Part of a transaction recorded in a journal or posted to a ledger.

**Equity:** The value of the business to the owner(s) of the business (which is the difference between the business's assets and liabilities). This is the same as the ownership interest, which consists of shares, retained profits and other reserves.

**Error of commission:** A double-entry term which means that one or both sides of a double-entry has been posted to the wrong account (but is within the same class of account). Example: petrol expense posted to vehicle maintenance expense.

**Error of omission:** A double-entry term which means that a transaction has been omitted from the books entirely.

**Error of original entry:** A double-entry term which means that a transaction has been entered with the wrong amount.

**Error of principle:** A double-entry term which means that one or both sides of a double-entry has been posted to the wrong account (which is also a different class of account). Example: petrol expense posted to fixtures and fittings.

**Expenditure (expenses):** Goods or services purchased directly for the running of the business. This does not include goods bought for resale or any items of a capital nature. Also referred to as expenses.

**Fiscal year:** The term used for a business's accounting year. The period is usually 12 months which can begin during any month of the calendar year.

**Fixed assets:** See *non-current assets*.

**Fixed cost:** A cost which remains stable within a relevant range of business activity.

**Fixtures and fittings:** This is a class of fixed asset which includes office furniture, filing cabinets, display cases, warehouse shelving and the like.

**General ledger:** See *nominal ledger*.

**Goodwill:** This is an extra value placed on a business if the owner of a business decides it is worth more than the value of its assets. It is usually included where the business is to be sold as a going concern.

**Gross:** Normally used with reference to sale or purchase price, meaning the price is inclusive of VAT.

**Gross loss:** The difference between sales and cost of sales, assuming cost of sales is greater.

**Gross margin:** The difference between the selling price of a product or service and the cost of that product or service often shown as a percentage: for example, if a product sold for 100 and cost 60 to buy or manufacture, the gross margin would be 40%.

**Gross pay:** Payment due to an employee before deductions such as taxes, social insurance, and health insurance.

**Gross profit:** The difference between sales and cost of sales, assuming sales is greater.

**Impersonal accounts:** These are accounts not held in the name of persons (i.e. they do not relate directly to a business's customers and suppliers).

**Imprest system:** A method of topping up petty cash. A fixed sum of petty cash is placed in the petty cash box. When the petty cash balance is nearing zero, it is topped up back to its original level again.

**Income:** Money received by a business from its commercial activities. See *revenue*.

**Income statement:** A financial statement made up of revenue and expense accounts which shows the current profit or loss of a business (i.e. whether a business has earned more than it has spent in the current year). Often referred to as a profit and loss account or P&L.

**Indirect cost:** A cost which cannot be specifically attributed to products or services.

**Insolvent:** A company is insolvent if it has insufficient funds (all of its assets) to pay its debts (all of its liabilities). If a company's liabilities are greater than its assets and it continues to trade, it is not only insolvent but, in the UK, is operating illegally.

**Intangible assets:** Assets of a non-physical or financial nature. An asset such as goodwill is a good example. See *tangible assets*.

**Invoice:** A term describing an original document either issued by a business for the sale of goods on credit (a sales invoice) or received by the business for goods bought (a purchase invoice).

**Irrelevant cost:** A cost which is not affected by a decision.

**Job costing:** A technique used to capture the full cost of a unit of output where units of output differ.

**Journal(s):** See *books of prime entry*.

**Journal entries:** A term used to describe the transactions recorded in a journal.

**Ledger:** A book in which entries posted from the journals are reorganised into accounts.

**Liabilities:** This includes bank overdrafts, loans taken out for the business and money owed by the business to its suppliers. Liabilities are included in the balance sheet and normally consist of accounts which have a credit balance.

**Liquidity:** The speed at which assets can be converted to cash.

**Long-term liabilities:** These usually refer to long-term loans (i.e. a loan which lasts for more than one year such as a mortgage).

**Loss:** See *net loss*.

**Management accounts:** Accounting information used by managers and directors of a business as opposed to financial accounts which are prepared for HMRC and any other parties not directly connected with the business. See also *cost accounting*.

**Memorandum accounts:** A name for the accounts held in a subsidiary ledger (e.g. the accounts in a sales ledger).

**Minority interest:** The portion of a subsidiary company not owned by a group.

**Narrative:** A comment appended to an entry in a journal. It can be used to describe the nature of the transaction, and often in particular, where the other side of the entry went to (or came from).

**Net:** Normally used with reference to sale or purchase price, meaning the price is exclusive of VAT.

**Net loss:** The value of expenses less sales assuming that the expenses are greater.

**Net pay:** The amount of employee pay remaining after all deductions.

**Net profit:** The value of sales less expenses assuming that the sales are greater.

**Net realisable value:** The sales value of an item held in stock, less any costs required to make the item saleable.

**Net worth:** See *equity*.

**Nominal accounts:** A set of accounts held in the nominal ledger. They are termed 'nominal' because they don't usually relate to an individual person.

**Nominal ledger:** A ledger which holds all the nominal accounts of a business. Where the business uses a subsidiary ledger like the sales ledger to hold customer details, the nominal ledger will usually include a control account to show the total balance of the subsidiary ledger (a control account can be termed 'nominal' because it doesn't relate to a specific person).

**Non-current assets:** These consist of anything which a business owns or buys for use within the business and which still retains a value over a number of years. They usually consist of major items like land, buildings, equipment and vehicles but can include smaller items like tools (see *depreciation*).

**Non-current liability:** A liability which will not be settled within one year. Typical examples are long-term bank loans or leases.

**Operating profit:** The amount of money generated by the normal trading activities of a business.

**Opportunity cost:** A cost which measures the loss or sacrifice of one course of action over another.

**Ordinary shares:** This is a type of share issued by a limited company. It carries the highest risk but usually attracts the highest rewards.

**Original book of entry:** A book which contains the details of the day-to-day transactions of a business (see *journal*).

**Overheads:** These are the costs involved in running a business and are normal business expenses (e.g. rent, insurance, petrol, staff wages, etc.).

**PAYE:** 'Pay as you earn'. The name given to the income tax system where an employee's tax and national insurance contributions are deducted before the wages are paid.

**Personal accounts:** These are the accounts of a business's customers and suppliers. They are usually held in the sales and purchase ledgers.

**Petty cash:** A small amount of money held in reserve (normally used to purchase items of small value where a cheque or other form of payment is not suitable).

**Posting:** The copying of entries from the journals to the ledgers.

**Preference shares:** This is a type of share issued by a limited company. It carries a medium risk but has the advantage over ordinary shares in that preference shareholders get the first slice of the dividend 'pie', but usually at a fixed rate.

**Pre-payments:** One or more accounts set up to account for money paid in advance (e.g. insurance, where part of the premium applies to the current financial year, and the remainder to the following year).

**Profit and loss account:** See *income statement.*

**Profit margin:** The percentage difference between the costs of a product and the price you sell it for. For example, if a product costs you £10 to buy and you sell it for £20, then you have a 100% profit margin. This is also known as your 'mark-up'.

**Pro-forma invoice:** An invoice sent that requires payment before any goods or services have been despatched.

**Provisions:** One or more accounts set up to account for expected future payments (e.g. where a business is expecting a bill, but hasn't yet received it).

**Purchases:** The cost of goods bought for resale or materials used to make a product.

**Purchase ledger:** A subsidiary ledger which holds the accounts of a business's suppliers. A single control account is held in the nominal ledger which shows the total balance of all the accounts in the purchase ledger.

**Raw materials:** This refers to the materials bought by a manufacturing business in order to manufacture its products.

**Receipt:** A term typically used to describe confirmation of a payment – if you buy some petrol you will normally ask for a receipt to prove that the money was spent legitimately.

**Reconciling:** The procedure of checking entries made in a business's books with those on a statement sent by a third person (e.g. checking a bank statement against your own records).

**Refund:** If you return some goods you have just bought (for whatever reason), the company you bought them from may give you your money back.

**Relevant cost:** A future cost that will change as a result of a decision.

**Reserve:** An amount of money put aside from profits to provide for items such as future expansion, acquisitions or guarding against future liabilities.

**Retail:** A term usually applied to a shop which resells goods. This type of business will require a trading account as well as a profit and loss account.

**Retained earnings:** This is the amount of money held in a business after its owner(s) have taken their share of the profits.

**Revenue:** The sales and any other taxable income of a business (e.g. interest earned from money on deposit).

**Revenue & Customs:** The government body usually responsible for collecting tax.

**Sales:** Income received from selling goods or a service.

**Sales invoice:** See *invoice*.

**Sales ledger:** A subsidiary ledger which holds the accounts of a business's customers. A control account is held in the nominal ledger (usually called a debtor's control account) which shows the total balance of all the accounts in the sales ledger.

**Service:** A term usually applied to a business which sells a service rather than manufactures or sells goods (e.g. an architect or a window cleaner).

**Shareholders:** The owners of a limited company.

**Shares:** These are documents issued by a company to its owners (the shareholders) which state how many shares in the company each shareholder has bought and what percentage of the company the shareholder owns. Shares can also be called 'stock'.

**Share capital:** The money obtained by a company from issuing shares to investors. Authorised share capital is the maximum amount of share capital a company can issue; issued share capital refers to the amount of share capital issued.

**SME:** Small and medium enterprises (i.e. small and medium sized businesses). The distinction between what is 'small' and what is 'medium' varies depending on context but there are distinct parameters with regard to regulations or grants.

**Sole trader/sole proprietor:** The self-employed owner of a business.

**Solvency:** The ability of a business to pay debts as they fall due. See also *liquidity*.

**Source document:** An original invoice, bill or receipt to which journal entries refer.

**Stakeholder:** A third party who affects, or can be affected by, the actions of a business. Stakeholders include managers, employees, suppliers, customers, shareholders and the local community.

**Stock taking:** Physically checking a business's stock for total quantities and value.

**Stock valuation:** Valuing a stock of goods bought for manufacturing or resale.

**Straight-line depreciation:** Depreciating something by the same (i.e. fixed) amount every year rather than as a percentage of its previous value. Example: a vehicle initially costs £10,000. If you depreciate it at a rate of £2,000 a year, it will depreciate to zero in exactly five years. See *depreciation*.

**Subsidiary company:** Within a group of companies, more than 50% ownership deems a company a subsidiary. It is assumed to be controlled or owned by the parent.

**Subsidiary ledgers:** Ledgers opened in addition to a business's nominal ledger. They are used to keep sections of a business separate from each other.

**Sunk cost:** A cost which has been made as a result of a prior decision and is irrelevant to any future decision.

**T account:** A particular method of displaying an account where the debits and associated information are shown on the left, and credits and associated information on the right.

**Tangible assets:** Assets of a physical nature. Examples include buildings, motor vehicles, plant and equipment, fixtures and fittings (see *non-current assets*).

**Trading account:** An account which shows the gross profit or loss of a business, i.e. sales less the cost of sales. It can be prepared before the profit and loss account, but is more often included as the first portion of the profit and loss account/income statement.

**Transaction:** Two or more entries made in a journal which when looked at together reflect an original document such as a sales invoice or purchase receipt.

**Trial balance:** A statement showing all the accounts used in a business and their balances.

**Turnover:** The income of a business over a period of time (see also *revenue*).

**Undeposited funds account:** An account used to show the current total of money received not yet banked. This can include money, cheques, credit card payments, banker's drafts, etc. This type of account is also commonly referred to as a 'cash in hand' account.

**Value Added Tax (VAT):** Value Added Tax, or VAT as it is usually called, is a sales tax which increases the price of goods. The current UK VAT standard rate is 17.5%, there is also a rate for fuel (heating fuels like coal, electricity and gas and not road fuels) which is 5%. VAT is added to the price of goods, so in the UK an item that sells at £10 will be priced at £11.75 when 17.5% VAT is added. VAT rates can alter.

**Variable cost:** A cost which increases in line with business activity.

**Wages:** Payments made to the employees of a business for their work on behalf of the business. These are classed as expense items and must not be confused with 'drawings'.

**Work in progress:** The value of partly finished goods.

**Write-off:** Depreciating an asset to zero.

# Index